Harper College Library

JUL   2009

3 2158 00466 7518

S0-BZI-246

DATE DUE

GAYLORD			PRINTED IN U.S.A.

Criminal Justice
Recent Scholarship

Edited by
Marilyn McShane and Frank P. Williams III

A Series from LFB Scholarly

Criminal Victimization of the Deaf

Lauren M. Barrow

LFB Scholarly Publishing LLC
New York 2008

HV
6250.4
.H35
B37
2008

Copyright © 2008 by LFB Scholarly Publishing LLC

All rights reserved.

Library of Congress Cataloging-in-Publication Data

Barrow, Lauren M., 1968-
  Criminal victimization of the deaf / Lauren M. Barrow.
      p. cm. -- (Criminal justice : recent scholarship)
  Includes bibliographical references and index.
  ISBN 978-1-59332-272-4 (alk. paper)
  1. Deaf--Crimes against--United States. I. Title.
  HV6250.4.H35B37 2008
  362.4'2--dc22

2008015988

ISBN 978-1-59332-272-4

Printed on acid-free 250-year-life paper.

Manufactured in the United States of America.

HARPER COLLEGE LIBRARY
PALATINE, ILLINOIS 60067

Table of Contents

List of Tables

List of Figures

Acknowledgements

I must thank so many people who encouraged, supported, assisted and believed in this project. Some key people are listed below but the list of individuals who inspired, motivated or helped me is endless. Please know that if not specifically listed, your contribution is known and deeply appreciated.

My deepest appreciation is extended to Professor Janet Duvall, Ohio University – Chillicothe Campus; Professor Barry Latzer, City University of New York – John Jay College of Criminal Justice and Dr. Andrew Karmen, City University of New York – John Jay College of Criminal Justice. I am truly and forever grateful for all of your patient encouragement, your faith in the project and the valuable contributions you provided during all phases of production.

I wish also to thank the individuals and institutions who shared their resources with me, Keri Lute, The New York Society of the Deaf, The National Technical Institute for the Deaf and Rochester Institute of Technology.

Thank you also to my family and friends who have listened ad infinitum to the ideas, edits, problems and solutions. In particular, my deepest thanks to Mrs. Melograna, Bill and Teri.

CHAPTER ONE

Society's Elements and the Deaf Experience

"The failings of the deaf people exist always in relation to the strengths of hearing people; moreover, deaf people are fantastically flawed in nearly all respects...; so it is clear that the purpose of the devaluation of the deaf person is to enhance the apparent value of the audist professional." (Lane, 1992: 72)

This quote eloquently states the foundation upon which this research is built. Whether or not it is true, or whether hearing people admit to it is not germane. What matters is that Deaf people believe it to be true. The history of oppression and denial of equality in society has led the Deaf to literally rebel against hearing infiltration of their world.

In May 2006, Gallaudet University students staged demonstrations and protests over the appointment of Jane K. Fernandes to the position of University President. Students at Gallaudet complained that Dr. Fernandes, who learned to sign when she was 23, did not communicate well in ASL. Since ASL is the cultural unifier for the Deaf, many doubted her ability to efficiently and effectively represent their community -- suggesting in part that she wasn't "deaf enough". Others claimed that their objections focused more on the fact that the presidential search process was seriously flawed, and that in their opinion, a proper search for the ideal candidate was never conducted. Whatever the basis for their objections, demonstrations, and protests, the end result was that on October 29, 2006, five months after the first protest, the Board of Trustees at Gallaudet University revoked the appointment of Dr. Fernandes as University President.

This is not the first time that Deaf students were victorious in changing the leadership of the University. Eighteen years ago, students forced the board to abandon its first choice of president, in favor of Dr. I. Jordan as Gallaudet's first Deaf president in more than 100 years. Emboldened by their most recent victory, protestors and students alike believe that the struggle for deaf rights is reinvigorated. According to Noah Beckman, president of the student government, the new search process must demonstrate "inclusion, transparency and equality", and students are looking for the next choice to be a more forceful advocate for deaf culture with a strong deaf identity (Schemo, 2006).

The problem: Criminal Victimization of Deaf Citizens

This research investigates an overlooked population of crime victims, the Deaf. It explores the nature and extent of criminal acts perpetrated against this vulnerable population. It identifies who is at greatest risk and defines the best methods for responding to their victimization. Further, and perhaps most importantly, it creates awareness and sensitivity of the reality of what happens when Deaf individuals become crime victims, and what **should** happen when such individuals are forced, through circumstances, to seek justice in a system structured for and controlled by the hearing community.

To determine the extent of criminal victimization, this study surveyed Deaf college students regarding their exposure to Part I offenses as defined by the Uniform Crime Report (excluding homicide). The questionnaire format used the National Crime Victimization Survey (hereinafter NCVS) as a model, but also borrowed elements from the

CAST-MR[1] as well as other surveys used with the Deaf population. Because of the specific nature of the primary language utilized by Deaf persons[2], this research modified the vocabulary and syntax to cater to the target population. This particular adaptation reflects sensitivity not previously employed when collecting data from Deaf persons.

A review of the published literature has shown a paucity of research into the arena of crimes against persons who are disabled generally, but specifically the Deaf. Although recent years have marked a growing awareness of this problem, the nature of the disability has now become the pivotal point on which to base specific research efforts in the future. There are no institutionalized reporting mechanisms for identifying the number of disabled persons in society (although efforts are underway to correct this, see Public Law 105-301[3]), and any attempt to measure the rate of crimes against the disabled have yet to be statistically tested and proven effective.

Data collection within the Deaf community presents many challenges on multiple levels, not the least of which is that most surveys are written in English and therefore are not easily understood by Deaf persons; additionally cultural barriers, specifically language and education, work to isolate the Deaf from mainstream society. This study makes a sincere effort to correct those shortcomings and gather

---

[1]   Everington, C.T. and Luckasson, R. (1992). *Competency Assessment to Stand Trial for Defendants with Mental Retardation (CAST-MR)*. International Diagnostic Systems, Inc.

[2]   This research acknowledges "person-first" syntax (wherein persons with disabilities prefer to have their personhood recognized before their disabling condition), but given the length and complexity of this document, the researcher chooses to employ traditional language structure when referring to the target population, i.e. Deaf persons.

[3]   The Crime Victims with Disabilities Awareness Act of 1998 directs the Attorney General to conduct a study on crimes against individuals with developmental disabilities. In addition, the Bureau of Justice Statistics must include statistics on the nature of crimes against individuals with developmental disabilities and victim characteristics in its annual National Crime Victimization Survey (P.L. 105-301).

valid, reliable data from persons who are Deaf, thereby filling a research void.

Research Objectives

This study examined many aspects of criminal victimization, including but not limited to the individual characteristics of the respondent, the environmental factors of the criminal incident, the relationship between victim and offender, the frequency surrounding the victimization, the level of the victim and offender's involvement with mainstream society, and the effectiveness of the criminal justice system responses.

Personal characteristics for each respondent were analyzed to better identify factors that might make someone more susceptible to criminal victimization. These were key elements for determining whether or not deafness contributed to target selection. The following questions were explored:

- How often were Deaf persons victimized?
- What types of crime presented the greatest risk to Deaf persons?
- Did victimization vary by race, age or gender?
- What was the prevalence of victimization in their lives so far?

Environmental characteristics for each incident were explored to better identify at-risk factors that might contribute to a criminal incident. Identification of these factors may also lead to the development of self-protective techniques or preventive training modules. The following questions were posed:

- Where were Deaf persons most at risk for victimization?
- Were Deaf victims targeted as a function of their disability?
- What was their relationship to their attacker(s)?

In an effort to measure the degree of mainstream involvement, this study included a short 15 question quiz inquiring about the respondents' familiarity with the basic functions, roles, and practices of the criminal justice system. It was devised to determine how much someone without formal training or education in criminal justice actually knew about the criminal justice system and its personnel. The rationale for inclusion arose from the belief that much of the average person's knowledge regarding the criminal justice system is acquired through pop culture and media outlets. Exclusion from the mainstream makes that knowledge difficult to acquire. The questions answered include:

- How influenced by the mainstream culture's portrayal of crime and criminal justice are Deaf persons?
- How accurate is the basic understanding of the criminal justice system by most Deaf persons?

By empirically identifying victim demographics, frequency of offenses, types of offenses, and basic awareness of criminal justice practices, all participants in the criminal justice system (including law enforcement personnel, prosecutors, judges, policymakers, etc.), as well as the periphery system involved in victim recovery (including counseling, funding and security personnel), will have greater awareness of how to best respond to a victim who is Deaf and also be able to effectively implement programs to prevent victimization.

Scope of the Research

This research will involve the collection and analysis of survey data from hearing students at Rochester Institute of Technology (hereinafter RIT), and Deaf students from Rochester Institute of Technology – National Technical Institute for the Deaf (hereinafter NTID). Additional materials for consideration include 1995-2002 crime data for college students derived from the National Crime Victimization Survey, as well as 2001-2002 Regional and National Summary of Deaf and Hard of Hearing Students 18 years of age and older from the

Gallaudet Research Institute (See Appendix A). The national data is limited to 18 - 24 year olds in order to comply with the age limitations imposed by both the John Jay College of Criminal Justice and the National Technical Institute for the Deaf Institutional Review Boards.

Theoretical Framework

Despite the acceptance that a relationship exists between disabilities and child abuse, very few researchers have attempted to construct a theoretical model to explain the phenomenon. Some work in this area has been done, (see Friedrich and Boriskin, 1978; Herrenkohl and Herrenkohl, 1981; Mullins, 1986); but findings did little to advance a causal model that clarifies whether abuse is a determinant or a by-product of a disability.

The first multi-disciplinary and integrated effort to explain why crimes are perpetrated against persons with disabilities is the Integrated Ecological Model of Abuse (Sobsey, 1994:159-162). Sobsey's model is guided by eight main elements that attempt to explain the nature of the relationship between a disabled individual and his/her care providers[4] but does not necessarily apply to the instant study since most persons who are Deaf do not require constant care and supervision.

Despite its limited application to this study, the model places great emphasis on the interactive relationship between a potential offender and a potential victim and the power inequities that exist. Those power inequities make a unique contribution to this study on a societal level. Since the Integrated Ecological Model is based in large part on Bronfenbrenner's Ecological Model (1977), this study will use Bronfenbrenner's model to develop a theoretical framework to analyze victimization within the Deaf community as it offers an opportunity to

---

[4]   (1) the potential victim; (2) the potential offender; (3) inhibitive and disinhibitive behaviors within the offender; (4) interactions between the potential victim and potential offender; (5) the relationship that determines those interactions; (6) social control agents; (7) the environment in which the interaction occur; and (8) the culture of the society that influences every interaction within it.

analyze the criminologic issues within a structure of society that illustrates the powerlessness of the population under study.

Outline of the Study

This research report is divided into six chapters. Chapter One introduces the problem of criminal victimization within the Deaf community, establishes a need for empirical analysis, and explains the evolution of the project. It also describes the extent of the problem, while keeping it in social context through recognition of the challenges presented by a subcultural identity. It explores the "anonymity" of the Deaf, not just within mainstream society, but also among other marginalized populations. Chapter One also discusses the unique challenges presented by this population that may serve to explain the virtual non-existence of studies in victimization literature.

Chapter Two provides a careful analysis of Bronfenbrenner's Ecological Model, exploring and explaining the four concentric zones of interaction in society with specific application to the Deaf community. It further explores the social and political construction of deafness from a subcultural vs. medical viewpoint and the current isolated and ostracized social position of the Deaf community. It also briefly summarizes the debate regarding whether or not deafness is, in fact, a disabling condition. This discussion is necessary to orient the reader to the reality of the Deaf experience. By appreciating the Deaf social position, one is better equipped to evaluate whether or not the criminal justice system is working justly and efficiently for all citizens.

Chapter Three introduces the origin of the study of victimology, explores contemporary victimological theories - first on a large scale involving general research findings, and then on a level specific to the Deaf community; and finally it summarizes the problem of victimization within the Deaf community for each of the index crimes studied herein.

Chapter Four provides a description of the research project in general, including an introduction to the research methodology used (Participant Action Research). It also provides a discussion regarding the survey instrument since it is important for the reader to understand why questions were posed using strong vocabulary and seemingly incorrect grammar. There is also a Table of Hypotheses to assist the reader in developing a conceptual understanding of this project; and finally, an explanation of the protective measures for each respondent is provided, ensuring the reader that respondent safety was of paramount consideration throughout this project.

Chapter Five provides a discussion of the findings concerning each of the hypotheses being explored within the structure of the victimological theories presented in Chapter Three. Drawing on the relative strength and stability of the findings, conclusions are made in terms of the extent to which the hypotheses have been proven, and where future criminological research should be directed.

And finally, Chapter Six discusses the foundational lessons learned from the overall study, presents policy recommendations for both the criminal justice system and the victim services field, examines the general and specific limitations of the instant study, identifies lessons learned unique to utilizing this survey instrument with the Deaf population, while making suggestions for future attempts at replication. It .closes with a discussion of the outlining what additional research is needed.

Deafness

It is important to understand certain terms within the Deaf-Hard of Hearing (HOH) community. To most individuals, being Deaf simply refers to one's inability to hear. Within the Deaf and hard of hearing community, however, being deaf has very specific meanings. Presented below are some of the more common terms used to identify this population, as well as a discussion regarding what meanings those terms hold within the Deaf community.

Hearing-Impaired is often used to describe an individual with limited hearing loss. It implies that one's ears [hearing] are medically broken or defective, and encourages the hearing community (audist professionals[5]) to "fix" the "brokenness". It ignores the fact that Deaf persons believe that by "fixing" deafness, their cultural identity will be eliminated, and they will be drawn into the mainstream with no recognition of their uniqueness.

Hearing-challenged and *hearing-disabled* are modern, more sensitive versions of the term "hearing handicapped". They evolved as the "politically correct" terms of identifying persons who couldn't hear very well. However, the community classifies these terms as weak replacements for Deaf and believes that they fail to change pre-existing stereotypes of "disabled" people as "weak, passive, dependent, unintelligent, worthless and problematic" (Galvin, 2003: 153).

Hard-of-Hearing (HOH) identifies individuals for whom "the sense of hearing, although defective, is functional with or without a hearing aid." Since there is no one generally agreed upon definition of hearing impairment, hearing disabled or hard-of-hearing, these terms often are used interchangeably, and typically include a qualifying adjective such as mild, moderate or severe (Gallaudet Encyclopedia of Deaf People & Deafness, 1987: 276). Persons who become deaf later in life as a function of aging are often included in this category, as it is unlikely they would learn a new language and further, that they would abandon their cultural identity upon becoming deaf.

Deaf (with a capital D) identifies individuals who are medically incapable of hearing (often pre-lingually[6]) and are active participants in the Deaf subculture. Persons who are Deaf represent a group who are

---

[5]   Audism represents the institutional response for dealing with deaf people, by making statements about them, authorizing views of them, describing them, teaching about them, governing where they go to school and, in some cases, where they live; in short, it is the hearing way of dominating, restructuring, and exercising authority over the deaf community. It includes such professional people as administrators of schools for deaf children and training programs for deaf adults, interpreters, and some audiologists, speech therapists, otologists, psychologists, psychiatrists, librarians, researchers, social workers, and hearing aid specialists (Lane 1992: 43).

[6]   Prelingual refers to deafness occurring before language acquisition.

proud of their deafness, use American Sign Language (ASL) as a primary means of communication, and employ no efforts to facilitate hearing. On the other hand, *deaf* (lowercase d) signifies individuals who medically are incapable of hearing but choose not to associate with other members of the Deaf community. Their deafness may also have occurred pre-lingually, but they differ from Deaf in that they attempt to *cure* their deafness through medical innovations such as hearing aids, cochlear implants, and/or amplifiers. They do not use ASL exclusively and sometimes are shunned by members of the Deaf community.

"Deaf" and "deaf" have very distinct meanings and will not be used interchangeably in this study. Hereinafter, the population will be referred to as d/Deaf to reflect inclusion of both the culturally Deaf population, and those who prefer to employ hearing assistive devices. Chapter Five will discuss further this study's success in gaining information from members of the Deaf community.

Evolution of Deaf Subculture

The 1970's ushered in an era of significant change in the United States. It was marked by minority groups, (such as African Americans, gays/lesbians, and women) asserting themselves and defending their lifestyle choices. Members of the Deaf subculture in America seized this era of change to reject the notion that they were diseased and in need of care and/or cure, and that their language was "deficient". The American Deaf language, American Sign Language (ASL) is borne of La Langue Signe Francaise (LSF). Both countries, America and France, were uniquely brought together by the united struggle to claim their identity as a minority group and be accepted by mainstream cultures as not necessarily disabled, just linguistically different. The significance of this struggle is only understood by a brief historical examination of Deaf subculture in both countries.

In 1779, the first book ever written by a deaf individual, Pierre Desloges, argued against the practice of forcing deaf children to speak French. He claimed that it masked a prohibition for them to speak at all (as cited in Lane, 1984). Simultaneously, Charles Michel (Abbé) de

L'Epée was promoting the development of a manual code that included a sign for every article of the French language.

In 1815, Thomas Gallaudet, a Protestant minister from Hartford, Connecticut, was sent by philanthropists to acquire the art of instructing Deaf people. He studied under Abbé Sicard (a disciple of Epée) with two others, Jean Massieu and Laurent Clerc. In the end, Gallaudet contracted Clerc to return to Hartford to assist in the establishment of the first public school for the Deaf in America, which became The Connecticut Asylum for the Education and Instruction of Deaf and Dumb[7] Persons.

Almost a century later at the French Exposition (1878) in Paris, a group of French educators affirmed the importance of spoken French language in deaf education (citing that to be denied hearing and speaking the French language is a tragedy), and advocated teaching deaf children through spoken language. Two years later, at the Milan Congress (1880) in Italy, a worldwide ban was placed on all signed languages. France responded by firing all Deaf teachers, out of fear that they would use La Langues des Signes Francaises (LSF) in their classrooms.

It wasn't until 1975, following the World Federation of the Deaf Conference in Washington, D.C., that France reintroduced the Deaf to their culture. At that conference French leaders were so impressed by the position that ASL had in American society that they began several programs aimed at the Deaf community in France, including the Total Communication (for classrooms), weekly television programs, development of an LSF dictionary, and the establishment of the Academy of French Sign Language at the Paris National Institute for Young Deaf People.

---

[7] "The 'dumb' of 'deaf and dumb' appears to refer not only to muteness but to weakness of mind." (Lane, 1992: 8). This perceived weakness of mind is believed to derive from the poor performance on standardized testing as described below.

In the 1990's several advances were being made in French society that greatly benefited the Deaf community and also attested to the success of their movement.   Some of the more notable accomplishments included an international conference on signed languages (Poitiers, 1990), bilinqual education for deaf children (Parliament, 1991) and the first European Conference on Deaf History held in 1992 (Rodez, 1992).

In April 1817, the Connecticut Asylum for the Education and Instruction of Deaf and Dumb Persons opened its doors in Hartford. The language used in the classroom was Clerc's manual French, signed language adapted to English.

As early as 1834, a single signed dialect was recognized in schools for the Deaf throughout the United States. It is surmised that the dialect originated from an evolutionary process that used Clerc's LSF as a foundation. It incorporated contact languages passed down through the generations following structural expansion through nativization, and finally, adjusting to a tendency to necessary grammatical regularization.   By 1869, over 1500 pupils had graduated from the Hartford school and were using the new signed language, which later came to be known as American Sign Language (ASL).

In 1857, Edward Gallaudet (son of Thomas) was asked to "take charge of and build up an Institution for the Instruction of the Deaf and Dumb and Blind in the District of Columbia" in accordance with directives "recently incorporated by an Act of Congress".   In 1862 Gallaudet wrote his benefactor, Amos Kendall, and pointed out that although "he provided for the admission of deaf and blind children....he had set no limit of time or age at which they must be discharged...and thus without intending to do so, [Kendall] had secured a very important provision of law for the starting of a college for the deaf." Hence, in 1864, the first college in the world for solely deaf students opened in Washington, D.C. (Gallaudet University).

However, the late nineteenth – early twentieth centuries heralded a significant paradigm shift regarding the education of deaf persons – the push towards oralism. Reports suggest that beginning in the 1870's and continuing through the mid-1970's, "ASL was never taught, was forbidden in the classroom, and was strongly discouraged outside of the school because the aim of deaf education for close to a century has been teaching the deaf to speak and to lip read" (Neisser, 1983: 3).

Progressives sought to reform education believing that it was responsible for preparing one for life and therefore held an obligation to push either practical subjects or vocational training; medical professionals, through technical innovations and medical treatments, sought to eliminate both the physical handicap of deafness and the social barriers of deaf persons; and social reformers sought to integrate America's marginalized populations and create cultural cohesion by enforcing a common spoken language (Burch, 2001:216).

Ironically, the Milan Conference (1880), the educational, medical, and social movements of the early twentieth century, and Alexander Graham Bell's[8] influence and support did little to "restore" deaf persons to the broader world, or to "normalize" them according to mainstream values (Burch, 2001: 216). Rather the efforts increased the degree of marginalization and isolation from mainstream culture and created a greater unity within the Deaf community that encouraged maintenance of a separate communal identity.

Isolated from social norms, united by their exclusion from lingual chauvinists[9], and bolstered by the development and support of the National Association of the Deaf (NAD)[10], the Deaf successfully

---

[8]   Alexander Graham Bell emerged as the greatest champion of oralism of all time, and therefore was identified as the "most feared enemy of the American deaf, past and present" (Lane, 1992: 340). He believed that normal society was made up of people who speak and hear, making use of the English language, and therefore, "that the job of educators [was] to prepare deaf children to make their way in the world, to use English, and to communicate in English by speaking and reading lips. Accomplishing this would "restore the deaf to society" (Gallaudet Encyclopedia, 1987: 137).
[9]   Term coined by this researcher to identify individuals or organizations who aggressively seek to suppress one's communication, in this case ASL, in favor of the dominate language, in this case English.
[10]   National Association of the Deaf (NAD) was organized in 1880 to serve as a national leader and crusader for the rights of deaf people. It advocates for the recognition of specific characteristics and unique differences that exist within the deaf community.

rebelled against the oralist model. First in France, where a group of hearing teachers staged a hunger strike to demand inclusion of deaf students and teachers (Poitiers, France, 1985); and then in Washington DC, wherein students and alumni protested the selection of a hearing candidate to serve as president of Gallaudet University (1988) and successfully demanded the placement of a Deaf president. It came to be known as the Deaf President Now[11] (DPN) movement.

While the Deaf have succeeded in asserting their identity and presence within society, the effects of social exclusion remain an everyday issue for this population. Their unique needs are seldom recognized by criminal justice personnel who deal, in general, with a non-physically handicapped, speaking population. Usually, such personnel lack the resources, communication skills, and training to effectively offer assistance to the Deaf.

Modes of Communication

Communication is a key indicator for determining immediately the degree of involvement with Deaf subculture – not unlike how an accent identifies a hearing person's regional origin. Three basic types of Deaf communication are listed below, each has unique language, comprehension and communication issues.

Oralists or Oral Deaf individuals have learned to speak and can communicate in English. They comprehend written and spoken English when pronounced in a clear and concise manner and with no over-pronunciation of the words. The mistake most often made with

---

[11]   The DPN supporters believed that the time had come for a deaf person to run the world's only university for deaf and hard of hearing students. When this didn't happen, the result was a protest whose effects are still reverberating around the world today.

   DPN was remarkable not only for its clear sense of purpose, cohesiveness, speed, and depth of feeling, but also for its ability to remove the barriers and erase the lines that previously separated the deaf and hearing communities. In addition, it raised the nation's consciousness of the rights and abilities of deaf and hard of hearing people.

Oralists is the assumption that because the hearing individual can understand the Oralist, the Oralist can understand the hearing person. This may or may not be true and is largely dependent upon factors such as facial features, gum chewing, moustaches, or the demeanor of the individual communicating.

Persons with minimal language skills use ASL and possibly some home signs. Regionalism and idioms will also be prevalent in their communications. Deaf in this group may have approximately a 1st to 3rd grade reading level, and communication will be difficult if one is not familiar with the cultural and geographic aspects of deafness.

Some d/Deaf individuals use definite signs. Some may be able to say a few words but could not carry on complete conversations. American Sign Language (ASL) and Signed Pidgin English (SPE) are examples of the sign languages utilized by this group. If ASL is used, there could be complications in writing and understanding on both sides, particularly since sign languages are geographically influenced. This results in a type of *regionalism*, where one word may have different signs, depending on the geographic location of the signing individuals. If SPE is used, the general context of the communication would be comprehended by both parties, but the overall communication may be slower.

The above mentioned factors, different communication methods, regionalized signs, and inaccurate lip-reading all contribute to the overall challenges that face d/Deaf victims when they are confronted by the criminal justice system. Add to these factors, the years of discriminatory practices and the general distrust of social control agencies by the Deaf community, and it is easy to understand why many victims choose not to report a crime. These elements provide the foundation for the hypothesis to be tested in this study that the "Deaf will be dissatisfied with the services from the criminal justice system". Further, such failings must be corrected if this population is to enjoy the same level of protection as other minority communities.

Methods of Sign Communication

The figures regarding individuals who have any level of hearing impairment range from 8,000,000 to 28,000,000 or (3.8% to 14% of the population respectively). Of those estimates, only 800,000 to 7,000,000 (or 0.4% to 3.4% of the population) are believed to be deaf, translated to mean "have difficulty hearing normal conversation". [12] Given those figures, it is relatively safe to assume that some percentage of Deaf persons will fall victim to a criminal incident. And yet, the challenges of communication between the Deaf and non-Deaf frequently preclude the possibility that a person who is Deaf will receive satisfactory service.

American Sign Language (ASL) is the official language of the Deaf community (in America). It uses one's hands to convey thoughts, feelings, and concepts in a systematic fashion. A direct sign-to-word translation is impossible since in many cases, individual signs do not translate accurately into English words. Basic knowledge of sign communication involves a familiarity of the five main elements used in signing: orientation, location, handshape, movement, and body language (Costello, 1994: xvii).

> *Orientation* of the palms refers to the direction of the palms, ie: up, down, left, etc. For example, an open palm facing outward means "your", whereas an open palm facing inward means "mine" and a slight bending of the fingers forward touching one's chest means "my".

> *Location* refers to where a sign is produced in relation to the signer's body. Just as a change in sound alters a word's meaning, so too, does a slight change in gesturing change a sign's meaning. For example, an upward motion of the index

---

[12]   Data from the report "How many deaf people are there in the United States" published by the Gallaudet Research Institute in 2004 (See Appendix C).

finger in front of shoulder (hand facing inward) indicates the number "11", while the same motion made at the temple means "understand".

Handshapes are also significant in the formation of a sign, i.e.,: open hand, curved hand, curved five, flattened C, etc.. For example, an open hand, facing the signer, gently tapping the chest means "mine", whereas a pointed index finger gently tapping the chest means "I".

Movement refers to the motion of the hand used to execute the sign. For example, an upturned fist (thumb up) moving away from the signer means "I help you"; whereas, the same sign used moving toward the signer means "you help me?".

Body language (nonmanual cues) is used very much the same way as in spoken language although in sign, its role is much more important, in that it sets the tone of the conversation. It is important, also, in that it functions to intensify feelings, modify verb actions, and index sequences.

When communicating in sign language, it is also important to know that the syntax of ASL differs significantly from English. Since, in its purest form, ASL does not utilize verb tense or qualifiers, it employs a time-noun-adjective-verb (TNAV) structure, rather than the noun-adjective-verb structure of English (Bone, 1998). While this may seem odd, the reality is that most people think in a TNAV format. For instance, consider for a moment how you would illustrate placing a book on a table. Most people would draw the table first because, without the table, the book would fall. Yet, when describing that activity verbally, one would say, "I put the book on the table". In ASL, the description would be "Now, table book on".

It is this key difference in syntax, added to the differences in vocabulary as limited by sign-to-word translation, that has resulted in many persons who are d/Deaf being considered "dumb". During the nineteenth century "dumb" was used in relation to animals to stress the lack of language in beasts and to affirm their stupidity (Branson & Miller, 2002). That same rationale led to the assumption that since severely or profoundly d/Deaf children could never be proficient in the dominant language, that the educational and vocational potential of a d/Deaf child was very basic, and they were destined for dumbness.

While American Sign Language is the main form of communication for the Deaf, there are several different types and styles of sign language that signal to another Deaf person how much the interviewer understands them and their subculture.

Signed Pidgin English (SPE) is foremost a means of communication, not a language. Since English and American Sign Language (ASL) differ significantly, SPE provides a way for hearing individuals who know a little signing to communicate with individuals who are Deaf. It is not perfect English, nor perfect ASL, but there are more signs used in SPE. The adaptation of ASL to SPE allows signing to occur in English format, making it more user-friendly to English speaking individuals. Other terms for SPE include Sign English, Ameslish and Siglish.

Signed Exact English (SEE) also represents a mode of communication, not a language. It is often most effective when communicating with a hearing person who is unfamiliar with signing because it mimics the syntax of English. However, it is awkward for use between Deaf and is not considered easy to read by persons who are Deaf. Other terms for SEE include: Total Communication (TC) and Manually Coded English (MCE).

Cued Speech is a visual communication system — mouth movements of speech combine with "cues" to make all the sounds (phonemes) of spoken language look different. When cueing English, eight handshapes distinguish consonant phonemes, and four locations near the mouth distinguish vowel phonemes. A handshape and a location together cue a syllable. The typical deaf cuer is flexible, able to communicate with speech, speechreading, Cued Speech, and signed language (NCSA, online).

Fingerspelling represents the American alphabet as written in air rather than on paper. There are 26 single-hand positions that represent each letter of the alphabet. It is generally used to support ASL, specifically in cases where there is no sign for a word or concept, where a sign may be obscure or idiosyncratic, when the receiver expresses doubt over the meaning of a word, or for common or personal names.

Communication is a major factor in working with any minority population. The identification of over twenty different communication modalities within the Deaf/HOH communities serves to further compromise the ability of a hearing individual to fully comprehend the situation unless significant effort and attention is directed towards the communication process. Further, in addition to the communication methods discussed above, other non-traditional forms of communication are often employed such as writing, gesturing (as with an anatomically correct doll[13]), or drawing.

The Deaf Community and the Criminal Justice System

The relationship between the Deaf community and the criminal justice system is complicated by the juxtaposition of law enforcement goals against the method of communicating by the Deaf. Sign language depends upon the transmission of ideas through the "visual" creation of an event and its situational environment. Transmitting this information entails quite a bit of time and includes greater detail than spoken words. This is of particular import when one encounters the "just the facts" approach of law enforcement. First responders are trained to quickly gather facts and assess the situation, leaving in-depth investigation of a criminal event to the detectives. However, the nature of Deaf communication is to provide rich detail about even small elements. That is often time consuming, labor intensive, and serves as an

---

[13] Goddard, M.A. (1989). *Sexual Assault: A hospital/community protocol for forensic and medical examination.* Rockville, MD: National Criminal Justice Reference Service.

obstruction to the goal of arrest, as it is believed by law enforcement that the longer the time interval between reporting and investigation, the less likely a perpetrator will be arrested (Greenwood and Petersilia, 1975).

Some law enforcement agencies seek to minimize awkward communication by using Telecommunication devices for the Deaf (TDD) or Relay services. Relay services involve a Deaf person using a TDD machine and having the text read aloud by a third party over the phone to law enforcement. The Deaf community complains that this third party violates their confidentiality, complicates the relationship between the police and victim, and denies them the opportunity to be certain that the information being transmitted is accurate (Sadusky & Obinna, 2002). The Department of Justice has also suggested that the use of the relay may not be appropriate in cases of crisis lines pertaining to rape, domestic violence, child abuse, drugs or organizations where people need confidentiality[14]. Although the relay operators have to sign a statement that they will keep all conversations confidential and are dismissed if they violate this confidentiality, the fact is that many people are reluctant to call through a third party in sensitive situations, including law enforcement situations.

The ideal situation is to have an interpreter present to communicate directly with criminal justice personnel and the Deaf victim. However, interpreters are not law enforcement, and therefore are not typically present when officers are responding to a call. Even with this ideal, having an interpreter does not guarantee accurate and coherent information, particularly in situations where the regionalism of the signing, use of home signs, or justice system signs are unfamiliar to the interpreter, the victim, or both[15].

---

[14]   Non-discrimination on the basis of disability in state and local government services. Office of the Attorney General, U.S. Department of Justice, Final Rule. 28 CFR Part 35 § 161.

[15]   A perfect example of this was experienced by the researcher of this project. When attending a conference for crime victims with disabilities in Riverside, CA (2002), the researcher learned a new sign for "victim" (a 'V'

The faith/trust issue holds even more importance in the specific relationship between the criminal justice system and the Deaf – that being, whether or not they choose to report crimes perpetrated against them. Moriarity (2002) suggested that crime victims, in general, feel that law enforcement officers failed to be sensitive or to provide them with critical information. With respect to vulnerable populations, she found that communities did not have adequate resources, training, or support programs in place to serve victims, thereby neglecting the needs of those who have already been victimized and minimizing the likelihood of future reporting" (Moriarty, 2002:52). So far, the perceived lack of sensitivity and understanding towards Deaf culture and language on the part of the criminal justice system – inadvertent though it may be – stands as an obstacle to equalizing the administration of justice.

---

waved in mid air of the dominant hand). When we were on site in Rochester, NY in early 2003, we used that sign to discuss "crime victim" and were queried by several Deaf as to the meaning of the sign. They had never seen it before.

CHAPTER TWO

Peeling back the layers of social discrimination

The reality of the Deaf as an isolated subculture is the end result of various exclusionary definitions that emanate from the dominant culture. This study will attempt to explain Deaf isolation as a function of constructed identities placed into a social context using Bronfenbrenner's ecological model. This isolation underscores the importance of discovering how serious the victimization problem may be, and finding out how the criminal justice system can more effectively serve this group.

By the end of the 19th Century, medicine and education emerged as hallmarks of a civilized society. American society had evolved from an agrarian community through the industrial age and emerged as a capitalist society. As such, it placed great cultural value on strong, intelligent, able-bodied individuals who could support themselves and their families, while simultaneously making positive contributions to the community. Below is a discussion of how cultural beliefs and attitudes are constructed from medical and educational classifications that result in the devaluation of persons with disabilities.

Social Construction of Deafness as a Disability

Social constructionism is an approach that focuses on *meaning* and *power*. It highlights the effects of social interactions on cognitive development revealing a critical role that external activities play in the development of mental constructs (Vygotsky, 1978). Understanding the interplay between the "internalization of what is outside, and the externalization of what is inside" is the heart of constructionism's paradigm (Papert, 1990:3).

With respect to this study, social constructionism is used to explain how disability is a "phenomenon *created by society* [emphasis added] (see Liachowitz, 1988; UPIAS, 1976:14). Social constructionism acknowledges the physical differences of a person, and even allows for a celebration of these differences. Ultimately, however, it shifts the focus away from the individual as the source of the "problem" and towards society's structures instead (Haller, 1999). It is a key element to understanding the cultural values of a community, and how cultural beliefs and attitudes survive over generations.

The Social Construction of Deafness in the United States

Americans believe that being Deaf is a tragedy. The tragedy centers on the division of society into two main ideological schools: one that construes "deafness" as designating a category of disability; the other that construes "deafness" as a relegation to an isolated linguistic and cultural minority (French-American Foundation, 1994:7). Both constructs require the division of society into groups: mainstream versus "disabled" or mainstream versus "subculture". Either way, the Deaf are removed from society and effectively labeled as different. This societal division marks the origin of the hypothesis in this study, that "the Deaf will demonstrate significant disenfranchisement from the criminal justice system". As a population separated from the mainstream, it is surmised that persons who are Deaf will feel disconnected from the legal and social control systems, in large part because they do not have easy, direct access to the assimilation processes of learning about society's social control institutions.

The disability construct associates deafness with silence; deprivation of a wonderful sense because of an inability to hear speech, music, and the sounds of nature; individual suffering; personal incapacities, and great obstacles to easy communication. Samuel Johnson is quoted as saying that deafness is "one of the most desperate of human calamities" (Sacks, 1989:1). This view, however, fails to recognize the unique and treasured identity of the Deaf subculture, and as a result, has created resentment from the d/Deaf[16] towards the hearing. Some advocates of Deaf subculture feel that the blame for attempts to obliterate their culture is limited to a specific group (audists[17]) who stand to personally benefit if deafness is "cured".

American d/Deaf have only just recently become conscious of themselves as guardians, not only of their own language, but also of their distinctive customs, values, and memories (Race, 1995). They want the rest of society to start showing respect for their culture. They have started asserting their right to be regarded as an "ethnicity", like Afro-Americans, rather than a subgroup of the disabled, alongside wheelchair users or the visually impaired.

The 'disability' (a/k/a Clinical-Pathological, Medical or Paternalistic) view accepts the behavior and values of people who can hear as

---

[16] The term "d/Deaf" is used as representative of the sample population and is inclusive of culturally Deaf students and those students who prefer to employ hearing assistive devices.

[17] Speech therapists and hearing-aid makers have a vested interest in relegating the Deaf to the status of a "disability group," and geneticists and ear surgeons are even worse: by providing counseling to couples said to be at risk of having deaf children, or offering cochlear implants as a cure for congenital deafness, they are in effect plotting the extermination of the Deaf. It is as a result of the recognition of this specific population of professionals that led to Harlan Lane's (1992: 91) clarification that "deaf people are angry with *audists* and not with hearing people". While this may be true in part, the resentment felt by the Deaf community against the hearing community is long-standing and is rooted in much more than the medical professionals' attempts to "cure" deafness.

"standard" or the "norm" and then focuses on how people who are Deaf deviate from that norm. It reinforces the view that Deaf people are deprived of one of the five senses, which results in paternalistic and oppressive behaviors and attitudes towards d/Deaf people. Such paternalism allows "disabled people [to] be treated as if they are the victims of some tragic happening or circumstance. This treatment will occur not just in everyday interactions but also will be translated into social policies which will attempt to compensate these victims for the tragedies that have befallen them" (Oliver, 1990:2). This *attempt to compensate* is, in effect, the foundation of a social welfare approach.

A related concept to the 'disability' construct is that of being "handicapped." A handicapped individual is generally described as one with a "deficiency, especially an anatomical, physiological, or mental deficiency that prevents or restricts *normal* achievement." It has a negative connotation which suggests social inferiority, hopelessness, and higher risks of poverty (Moore, 1993:180) which is contradictory to the fact that many d/Deaf people live a full life, work, pay taxes, and positively contribute to society. From mainstream society, the label solicits pity, *not respect,* and further isolates the d/Deaf community. This study will raise the issue of whether deafness is a "handicap" or a "disability" that leads to greater vulnerability to crimes like assault, robbery, and rape.

Alternatively, the cultural-minority construct views the d/Deaf community as a group of persons who share a common means of communication (most often sign language) that provides the basis for group cohesion and identity. Deafness is associated with a unique language, history, culture, social group, and set of social institutions.

The cultural perspective is a view that is generally held by the Deaf about the Deaf. Even so, "deaf culture" as a conscious force is still in its early stages, creatively changing and ever-evolving. While some members of the d/Deaf community prefer to identify themselves not as a totally distinct culture, but as a sub-culture within mainstream society, similar to the Hispanic or Asian[18] subcultures (Moore, 1993: 220), advancements in the medical community resulted in cultural shifts where deafness became a disability that could be cured. However, staunch advocates of Deaf subculture do not seek assimilation into a "spoken" English or mainstream society, and reject medical contributions, such as surgical repairs or cochlear implants. They may also be unusually reluctant to turn to the authorities for help.

Regardless of whether one accepts the medical or cultural construct, the more important discussion is how deafness is used to *push* an individual out to the periphery of mainstream society, and how that process of marginalization has evolved from a simple linguistic difference into a chronic reality of social discrimination.

Young (2001) reported that employed Deaf people tend to occupy the lower-status, lower-paying positions, despite the fact that their presence may be essential. In her study, where one-third of the staff were Deaf, more than 90% of them were working at "unqualified" grade levels, having no access to professional education, and were not expected to advance to "qualified" levels. This unfair power differential, with its roots in both frank and unconscious discrimination, contributes to misunderstanding and resentment. Deaf staff often report feeling under-valued and isolated, as well as unsure of their skills because of gaps in their training. Some see themselves as members of a minority group in a hearing world that plans, organizes, and controls their activities.

---

[18] However, a significant difference between the Deaf and other linguistic minorities is the added barrier of not being able to hear (or to have limited hearing) the spoken English language (Holcomb & Peyton, 1992). As it is, most Deaf high school graduates comprehend written English at roughly a third or fourth grade level as determined by standardized reading assignments (Allen, 1986; King & Quigley, 1985; Tucker, 1991). In their writing, they often make vocabulary and structural errors that include omitting or confusing articles, prepositions, and verb tense markers, and they have difficulty with complex structures such as complements and relative clauses (Swisher, 1989).

Bronfenbrenner's Ecological Model

The ecological model (Bronfenbrenner, 1977) uses a series of concentric zones to describe child development as an accommodation to immediate environments within which direct interaction takes place and proceeds to increasingly distant levels of the social world that affect child development. This section introduces the zones of Bronfenbrenner's model from the inside out: the microsystem (intimate contact/ interaction, ie: parent-child); the mesosystem (interaction with family unit, i.e.: work, school); the exosystem (social institutions, i.e.: criminal justice, religion and politics); and the macrosystem (cultural attitudes, beliefs and values). This study adapts Bronfenbrenner's model from child development to one of social application in an effort to provide a foundation upon which one can begin to understand Deaf people and their placement in society. It further explores how those elements function together to render the Deaf socially and economically disadvantaged, and therefore, politically less powerful than their numbers would imply.

Finally, this study traces how these "disadvantages" affect crime and justice concerns, such as how effective are interpretive services throughout case processing? Or, is there a resistance to protect victims who are Deaf when the offender is also Deaf? Or, is there an inability to provide victim assistance to victims who are Deaf due to limited resources or lack of trained personnel?

Microsystem – Intimate Contact

The microsystem refers to situations in which the child has face-to-face contact with influential others, mainly represented by family members, peers, teachers, etc. In situations where a Deaf child is born to hearing parents, a multitude of issues can arise on both cultural and individual levels. The reality that over 90% of children born deaf are born to hearing parents, most – if not all --of whom do not know sign language, profoundly affects the process of language acquisition, and ultimately, cultural inclusion. Studies indicate that by age four, a hearing child of hearing parents has a vocabulary of 5,000 words; by comparison, a deaf child of hearing parents, at age four, has a vocabulary of only 50 words.

The learning deficit and resultant exclusion from verbal society often continues through adulthood and into old age (www.nhdeaf-hh.org/svc_fslp.html).

Further, hearing parents may deny their children access to Deaf subculture, or parents and siblings may choose not to learn sign language or may trust the input of the medical community to "fix" their child[19]. Historically, Deaf children were sent to live in residential settings with other Deaf. While these settings were believed to be critical to the survival of Deaf subculture, they required that parents relinquish their children to institutional settings which only increased the child's sense of alienation and isolation from his or her family.

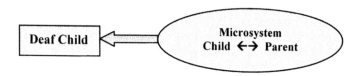

The Enlightenment period of the 18th Century heralded a rational and scientific approach to religious, social, political, and economic issues that promoted a secular view of the world and a general sense of progress and perfectibility (www.bartleby.com/65/ en/Enlighte.html). With respect to d/Deaf life, this "perfectibility" resulted in a drive towards oralism as a means of assimilation into mainstream society. Parents were eager to "normalize" their deaf children by teaching them to communicate in "spoken" language by lip-reading – but the hearing consistently fail to realize that an ability to speak does not equate to an ability to hear. If parents resist learning sign language, then communication is one-sided. Not knowing how to communicate with other Deaf may prevent parents from becoming aware of existent risk factors, and introduces an obstacle to communicating self-protective measures to their children, which further exposes a child who is Deaf to risk.

---

[19] (for a more in depth analysis of these issues, see Crouch, 1997)

Therefore, the fundamental level of social attachment that hints at security and acceptance becomes irreparably flawed if the child who is Deaf is denied bonding and communication with family members. From this fractured beginning, the rest of Bronfenbrenner's model seems unimportant and simply acts to increase the d/Deaf person's exposure to personal risk.

Mesosystem – Interaction with family units

The *mesosystem* encompasses the relationships with institutional elements that interact with the family unit (e.g., school and work) but does not necessarily have direct influence on family decision-making practices. It is important to note that with respect to this study, the mesosystem marks the beginning of the significant impact generated from macrosystemic elements of cultural attitudes and beliefs. The cultural perception (as developed by the educational and employment arenas) that disabled people is flawed in some way and will never be able to contribute positively to society. This may explain why few criminal justice officials or agencies have shown an interest in taking the extra measures needed to effectively serve this community. Since most of the cultural elements (macrosystemic) and the social institutions (exosystem) are the same for all members of society, this level commands significant discussion because it is in the educational and employment arenas where the specific value afforded to an individual or to a group becomes identified.

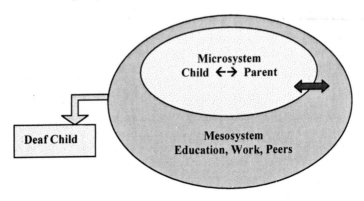

Education

Chapter One discusses the evolution of Deaf subculture in the United States and introduces the conflict between the manualists and the oralists. This information provides a foundation for understanding the importance of how the Deaf learn, but fails to explain why education has dominated discussions of socialization in the Deaf community for so long. The reason is quite simple, for the most part d/Deaf students are being graduated from both residential and mainstreamed programs with a third-grade reading levels. That translates into little chance of going to college or ever holding more than a minimum-wage job (Halpern, 1997). These limitations, in turn, expose the d/Deaf to many factors (identified and discussed in detail in Chapter 3 below) conducive to victimization.

During the early twentieth century, formal education became the agent of normalization in Western societies (Branson and Miller, 2002). Children were classified as either "normal" or "feebleminded" on the basis of an IQ test developed by Alfred Binet and Theodore Simon in 1905 and translated into English by Henry Goddard in 1908. While this test was initially developed to assist "slower" students to achieve their greatest human potential, it soon evolved into an instrument used to advance the eugenic goal of identifying and removing "idiots" from society. In 1913 Goddard was invited to Ellis Island to help detect morons in the immigrant population. In his *Intelligence Classification of Immigrants of Different Nationalities* (1917), he asserted that most of the Ellis Island immigrants were mentally deficient. For example, he indicated that 83% of all Jews tested were feeble-minded, as were 80% of the Hungarians, 79% of the Italians, and 87% of the Russians. The result was that many immigrants were turned away and sent back to Europe (Dakwa, 2001).

Since language proficiency is critical to performing well on IQ tests, d/Deaf people have consistently performed poorly (see footnote #12, pg. 31 herein). Under Goddard's model, their poor performance classified them as "idiots" and "uneducable," which resulted in their segregation from [normal] society into homes for the "mentally defective" (Branson and Miller, 2002), and ultimately a perception of "dumb".

Although Goddard's work was ultimately rejected, and oralism was deemed a "dismal failure" (Congressional Babbidge Report, 1965), mainstream culture continued to rationalize and assert superiority over less intellectually capable people. The advent of Total Communication methods (TC) coupled with Public Law 94-142[20] (1975) heralded the move towards mainstreaming disabled students into public education. Faced with the opportunity to keep their children home, and have them engage in the culture and language of their families, many parents welcomed the chance to mainstream their children who were Deaf.

Traditionally, deaf residential schools are well known as the bastions of Deaf culture, and most d/Deaf children who attend them eventually learn ASL and develop lifelong relationships. Unfortunately, deaf residential schools are often sorely deficient in actual education. The teachers rarely use ASL or are not often required to teach Deaf history. The administrations, often hearing people, place considerable academic focus on "word attack" and speech skills, rather than science, math, history, and English literacy (Halpern, 1997). As a result, many d/Deaf students graduate from residential institutions barely literate (Farwell, 1976:19)[21].

Congress dealt a final blow to residential institutions when they amended the Individuals with Disabilities Education Act from 1972 and recommended that disabled students should be in the "least restrictive environments". The Act labeled Deaf residential institutions as *Most Restrictive Environments,* and many residential schools were forced to close as enrollment quickly declined.

The 20th century embraced sign language as a communicative method that hastened the demise of segregation and allowed children to be mainstreamed as "disabled" students. Really, it only succeeded in shifting the paradigm from intellectually incapable to medically inferior – effectively leaving normate superiority intact. The medical

---

[20]   Public Law 94-142 required that handicapped children in the United States be provided free and appropriate education.
[21]   Research suggests that this is based upon 60% of the adult Deaf population that graduated which assumes that 40% did not graduate and one can expect to lower literacy levels in that population.

perception of inferiority has cultural implications that actively work to isolate and remove those so identified from society, which, in turn, has criminal justice implications.

Resnick (1984) writes that the social isolation or devaluing of an individual leads to the acceptance of a restricted role in society, which works to create a "sociological destiny" for the person with a disability. Such a destiny often dictates lower educational attainment, greater non-employment, lower wages when they are employed, and a lack of upward mobility. These findings affirm the intricacy of the institutional relationships on the mesosystemic level. With respect to the instant study, victimization surveys have consistently suggested that low income persons face greater risks of suffering from both violent and property crime.

Work / Employment

People who are disabled are likely to face exclusion from the workforce (Oliver, 1990:86) [22]. The resulting economic deprivation serves only to create a poverty-stricken population made up, in large part, of persons with disabilities, ultimately contributing to "...structural unemployment and other social problems" (Karmen, 1996:18).

One such "social problem" is that persons with low-paying jobs are often forced to rent apartments in low income/low rent neighborhoods. Victimization surveys reveal that low income neighborhoods are also typically high crime areas. Should victimization result, it serves only to reinforce the perception (as created by the powerful classes) that persons who are Deaf are unable to take care of themselves and thus creates an environment where the wealthy can justify their domination as those with the ability to "fix" what is broken, i.e.: using medical technology to "cure" the deafness.

---

[22] Census 2000 disability-related questions queried (#16a) "Does this person have any of the following long-lasting conditions? Blindness, deafness, or a severe vision or hearing impairment?"

People answering affirmatively to this question were classified as having a physical disability.

It is important to note that the subject of employment within the disabled population has become one of dynamic change since the passage of ADA in 1992. At that time, the definition of "disabled" was legally determined for purposes of access to public programs. Since ADA guidelines are based on the NAGI[23] (1969) framework, the directives of ADA recognize that improvements in the environment (access to public transportation, workplace accommodations, etc.) can reduce disability and thus improve the inclusion of all people. Preliminarily, this would appear, based on the SSI data, to actually be happening; however, the Deaf suffer from an ingrained discrimination based on the fear associated with the linguistic chauvinism of hearing people.

Sadly, the outcome of those behaviors has led to schools, job sites, health and service providers, and others in completely failing to address the unique communication needs of people who are d/Deaf[24]. This failure has severely limited Deaf access to education, employment, health care, legal, and other mesosystemic institutions and their services. The result is a disproportionate rate of poverty, unemployment, illiteracy, mental illness, substance abuse, and family dysfunction among persons who are Deaf. According to the National Association of the Deaf statistics, 80% of all deaf people receive Social Security Assistance (www.nhdeaf-hh.org) and in the state of Washington, approximately 65% of the 14,000 profoundly Deaf citizens have incomes at or below the federal poverty level (www1.dshs.wa.gov/hrsa/odhh).

---

[23] Nagi, S. Z. (1969). *Disability and Rehabilitation*. Columbus, OH: Ohio State University Press.

[24] A Deaf woman told the group she can't get job interviews when she says in application letters that her prospective employer must provide her with an interpreter (Spector, 2002).

Data from the CPS shows no significant improvement in the economic well-being of Americans with disabilities from 1989 through 1994[25] (McNeil, 1995).

Exosystems – social institutions

The third layer of analysis is the exosystem, which is represented by environments or social units (i.e.: social control agents, politics, religion) that may have direct or indirect influence on the primary unit – in this case, the Deaf.

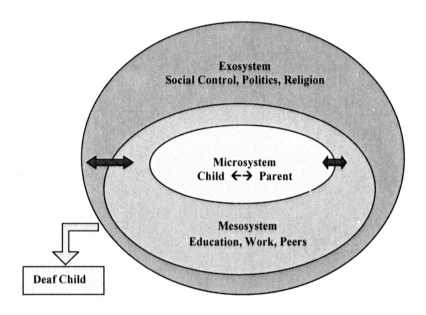

Law enforcement and criminal justice

---

[25]   29 percent of working-age adults limited in their ability to work lived in poverty in 1989 and in 1994, the poverty rate was more or less the same, at 30 percent.

The relationship between the Deaf and the criminal justice system is challenging and confusing. If an individual who is Deaf enters the system as an offender, then the language of the criminal justice system can be inherently insensitive ("You have the right to remain silent"). Further, justice practices such as handcuffing one's hands behind the back effectively renders the Deaf speechless and only serves to isolate, oppress, and instill fear in the Deaf. The general distrust and fear among the Deaf population, with respect to the justice system, has a direct effect when they must call upon that system for assistance.

Since persons who are Deaf can be victims, suspects, defendants, or prisoners, it would seem that the government should have an obligation to adapt its programs and policies to meet the linguistic needs of the Deaf. In reality, the government's obligation is to protect from discrimination and to provide equal access to remedies for discriminative practices. The Americans with Disabilities Act (ADA) represents the "federal government's most recent and extensive endeavour to address discrimination against persons with disabilities", but the Act has been interpreted as "not requiring a public entity[26] to provide any particular service" (Wooster, 2000:637-87).

Logically, the enormity and difficulty of the communication process between the Deaf and the hearing can preclude a Deaf victim from receiving satisfactory service, but whether the unsatisfactory service rises to the level of violation worthy of Court intervention is another issue; for example, a violation was found wherein a Deaf arrestee was denied (despite requests) alternatives to a conventional telephone, and therefore, was unable to post bond or make a telephone call for assistance;[27] whereas, the humiliation and embarrassment experienced by a Deaf arrestee resulting "from police failure to have and use

---

[26] "Public entity" is inclusive of a state or local government, including departments, agencies and other instrumentalities of the state and local government.
[27] Hanson v. Sangamon County Sheriff's Dept., 991 F.Supp. 1059 (C.D. Ill. 1998).

auxiliary communication aids" did not constitute an ADA violation[28] (Wooster, 2000: 671).

Politics

The American political scene is unique in that it affords everyone a degree of control (or at least the appearance of such) to the extent that they choose to actively participate in the development and selection of policy. Exclusion from the political arena often results in functional eradication. Without a voice or political presence, it becomes quite difficult for a group with common issues to be heard regarding their specific needs. A brief description of key political philosophies is presented below with reference to the influence on the criminal justice system and attitudes towards victimization.

During the late 1960's, when street crime rates were alarmingly high, and key judicial decisions (see *Miranda v. Arizona, Terry v. Ohio and Mapp v. Ohio*) resulted in offenders getting released on "technicalities", the average, law-abiding citizen became fearful for his safety.

Political conservatives responded to this fear with an agenda aimed at preventing crime (deterrence) through swift, certain, and severe punishment of offenders. Victim usefulness within the conservative ideology is as a witness for the state against a defendant, not necessarily as an individual who requires rehabilitative services and treatment for his or her injuries. Recognition that victims require rehabilitative services falls more in line with liberal philosophy, which shifts focus away from offender punishment and towards victim restoration to pre-victimization status (Anderson and Newman, 1998).

The Liberal agenda places significant value on individual rights and on protecting those rights from the power of the government through legal processes. The rehabilitative obligation originates from the social

---

[28] Rosen v. Montgomery County Maryland, 121 F.3d 154, 24 A.D.D. 902, 7A.D. Cas. (BNA) 70 (**4th Cir**. 1997).

contract theory[29] (Hobbes, 1651; Locke, 1689), wherein, if the government fails to provide a safe and secure existence (after citizens relinquish certain inalienable rights in return for a safe existence), then the government has a responsibility to restore the citizen to pre-victimization status.

Such responsibilities are presented in the phrase "equal protection of the laws,[30]" which implies that all persons, whether victim or defendant, are provided for equally by the law. However, the laws, as written, can not adjust to meet specific physical and lingual needs of all citizens. Therefore, the reality for persons with disabilities is that while laws do exist to protect them, without special adaptation that recognizes the uniqueness of the individual and their abilities, such protections represent, instead, an empty and unavailable promise.

Radical (critical) ideology argues that only a small proportion of the populous has enough political and economic power to control the definition of criminal behavior imposed upon the rest of society. This power serves a dual purpose of preserving the status of the wealthy and justifying the use of control and coercion to maintain social order (Anderson and Newman, 1998).

---

[29]   Thomas Hobbes (1588-1679) contended that people relinquished some of their individual rights to the state, in return for their protection and a more functional society, arguing therefore that social contract evolved from interests of self-preservation through soveriegn intervention. Alternatively, Locke's social contract theory was intertwined with his understanding of an innate, essential human rationality constituting 'natural law'. It is said that Locke believed that man is naturally good, and is not solely driven by greed and evil. It could be argued that Locke's theory rests on the presumption that moral values are widely shared independent of governmental intervention. For this reason, he is considered (especially on the American side of the Atlantic) one of the main thinkers of liberalism.

[30]   With respect to persons with disabilities, equal protection legislation is also criticized for contributing to a paternalistic attitude and/or perpetuating the stereotype of persons with disabilities as unable to protect themselves (Sobsey, 1994:276)

Radical ideology is uniquely applicable to this study in that the Deaf represent a powerless minority. They are, in effect, victimized by the social construction of Deafness as a disability and by society's failure to recognize their cultural identity. The result of this dilemma is that the Deaf are excluded from mainstream culture, and as such, have no power base from which to effect social change. Fry (1987) found that many disabled people did not even appear on the electoral register; specifically, the deaf and blind were denied access to all information necessary to make an informed choice. The problems seemed insurmountable to the point that many persons with disabilities, Deaf included, often choose not to exercise their rights to vote.

Religion

Evans-Pritchard (1937) suggested that "in societies dominated by religious or magical ways of thinking, disability is likely to be perceived as punishment by the gods or individual disabled people [are] to be seen as victims of witchcraft". Some cultures "frown on malformed children, whose existence is often attributed to the sins of a past life" (Hitchens, 2006:108). While this negative interpretation exists in some societies, others may view an individual with differences as "being chosen, as being possessed by a god, and consequently, the person may have their [social] status enhanced[31]" (Oliver, 1990:23).

With respect to deafness, mystical properties and secret communications have added a curious dimension[32] to the role of religion (or theology) in social acceptance. Initially, it was believed that in order to be "saved", one must be able to "hear" the word of God,

---

[31]   "Throughout history, discriminatory practices against the sick and disabled vary greatly from country to country and from century to century; they range from compete rejection and ostracism to semideification and the according of special privileges and honors." (Safilios-Rothschild, 1970: 4)

[32]   "Children who are deaf are a bit like angels. To communicate with them, give them instructions, comfort them with kind words, read stories to them — requires a special soundless language, the language of signing. Not surprisingly, it's sometimes referred to as the "language of angels." (Morrone, 2001)

and so people born deaf could not have faith, could not be saved, and were therefore barred from churches. Such primitive thinking no longer prevails, yet religious exclusion is still a reality for many Deaf. Few religious organizations or institutions offer services in sign language, resulting in the perception that Deaf communication needs cannot (or will not) be met. The result is, as expected, that the Deaf feel excluded, or more importantly, unwanted by organized religion. This is illustrated in verses such as the following:

> *Do angels sing in heaven, Lord? Will I hear music there?*
> *Or must I stand in a corner, While others join in prayer?*

> *Will I wonder what they're saying, Lord? Like I often do down here?*
> *Must I sit still and be patient, While bells ring loud and clear?*

> *Can I read your lips in heaven, Lord? Or will I be brushed aside?*
> *Will I hide my hands in my pocket, Because of wounded pride?*
> From the "Deaf Christians Prayer"

Macrosystem – Cultural Attitudes, Beliefs and Values

Bronfenbrenner's macrosystem represents the overarching institutions, practices, and patterns of beliefs that characterize society as a whole, while simultaneously considering input from the smaller micro-, meso-, and exosystems. Most specifically, the elements of the macrosystem are cultural values, beliefs and attitudes.

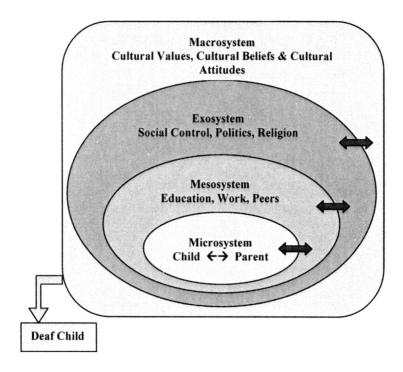

Cultural values are culturally defined standards by which people assess desirability, goodness and beauty (Macionis, 2001:67). Of the ten values central to American life[33] (Williams, 1970), the most applicable to this study is "racism and group superiority" wherein Williams claims that "...[o]ur society values males above females, whites above people of color, people with Northwest European backgrounds above those

---

[33] (1) Equal opportunity; (2) Achievement and Success; (3) Material comfort; (4) Activity and work; (5) Practicality and efficiency; (6) Progress; (7) Science; (8) Democracy and free enterprise; (9) Freedom; (10) Racism and group superiority.

whose ancestors came from other lands, and rich people above poor."
Were one to be devalued on any level, their intrinsic usefulness is
called into question by society because survival (both on a cultural and
an individual level) has often been tied intimately to a Darwinistic
philosophy of "only the strong will survive".

First and foremost, cultural beliefs are specific statements that people
hold to be true and are the foundations upon which rules defining
acceptable cultural practices are built. Western culture is challenged by
changing social mores and customs, particularly in countries where
several cultures converge. In such environments, society is faced with
providing a philosophical foundation for the development of
contemporary, cultural beliefs. Such beliefs also dictate guidelines for
rituals, ceremonies, and prohibitions that are viewed as vital to the
continuation and survival of a culture. For instance, American cultural
history favors qualities that support an individual's ability to contribute
positively to social welfare, such as self-reliance, rugged individualism
and success. Individuals who fail to conform to standards of physical
strength, social expectation, and medical fortitude are seen as burdens
on society that threaten the cultural infrastructure.

Culture generally refers to a body of learned beliefs, traditions, and
guides for behaving and interpreting behavior that are shared among
members of a particular group. It includes values, beliefs, customs,
communication styles, behaviors, practices, and institutions. The visible
aspects of a culture include clothing, art, buildings, food; the less
visible aspects of culture include values, norms, worldviews, and
expectations (Blue, 2005). Once a culture has identified specific
behavioral values and beliefs, and those expectations are communicated
to members of society, then ingrained cultural attitudes evolve as
reflections of those cultural expectations. Such may be the genesis of
the attitudes that people with disabilities are unable to provide for
themselves, and therefore, become a burden to society.

The cultural values, beliefs, and attitudes discussed above work to
create an infrastructure within which society shapes its relationships
and interactions with others. It orients the reader to the social attitudes
towards persons with disabilities generally and persons who are Deaf

specifically; and finally, provides a foundation upon which to understand the developing structure of this report.

Bronfenbrenner's model effectively illustrates how society fails on both an individual level and a societal level to include persons who are Deaf and embrace their differences. Any effort to equalize the administration of justice to this population requires major paradigm shifts at every level of society before that equality can be realized.

CHAPTER THREE

Deaf persons as victims

"I am sickened to know that generations of people with disabilities are raped, beaten, and killed. My disgust is compounded by the scant attention that domestic and sexual violence professionals are paying to this issue. There is a serious lack of interest and commitment to examining how and why domestic and sexual violence is complicated for people with disabilities. I find no evidence of a meaningful effort to make our services accessible, practical resources for people with disabilities. The effect of our intentional choice is shameful and telling."
Joelle Brouner, Project Action Community Organizer
January 2001

It stands to reason that as long as there has been crime, there have been victims. However, as an area of scientific exploration, victimology has failed to achieve recognition as much more than a "chapter" within the broader discipline of criminal justice. Identification as a "science" is challenged by the lack of a theoretical foundation, definitive operationalization of the term "victim", and little empirical support for any theory that does exist.

Before the 1940's, criminology primarily focused its research efforts on the criminal perpetrators and their acts. It wasn't until the 1950's that two criminologists, Mendelsohn and Von Hentig, began to study the role of the victim in the offender/victim dialectic relationship. They are now considered the "fathers of the study of victimology" (Roberson, 1994). The title of "father" is shared because each approached their investigations from different perspectives: Mendelsohn explained victimization situationally by focusing on the relationships between victim and offender, while von Hentig focused on personal characteristics such as one's social, psychological, or behavioral mannerisms that contributed to victimization.

Fathers of Victimology[34]

The first mention of crime victims as a potential area of inquiry occurs during an investigation into the relationship between rape victims and their assailants by Benjamin Mendelsohn (1963). His typologies of victim as described by Schafer (1968) included the (1) *innocent victim* – where the victim was unconscious of or unaware of their potential for victimization; (2) *victim-precipitated victimization* – where the victim somehow contributed to his/her own injury; (3) *victim with minor guilt* – where victimization occurs as a result of where or with whom individuals choose to spend their time; (4) *victim as guilty as offender* – where the victimization occurs as part of a criminal act; (5) *victim is more guilty than offender*– where the victim acts first to provoke or attack an individual and ends up injured, and finally, (6) *most guilty victim* – where victim is killed after provoking an attack.

---

[34]   The concept of victim dates back to ancient cultures. Its original meaning was based in the idea of sacrifice – the execution of a person or animal to satisfy a deity or hierarchy. Victimologists initially used the word victim to refer to hapless dupes who instigated their own victimizations, but this ideology was abandoned because of the "victim blaming" tendencies and was replaced by the idea of someone caught up in an unbalanced, exploitative, parasitical relationship that had inherit suffering. In this view, victimology refers to power differentials.

Currently the term "victim" refers to any person suffering injury, loss or hardship for any reason, i.e.: cancer, Mother Nature, injustice; while "crime victim" generally refers to any person, group, or entity who has suffered injury or loss due to illegal activity. The harm can be physical, psychological, or economic. (http://faculty.ncwc.edu/toconnor/300/300lect01.htm)

Mendelsohn's suggestion that victims were complicit in their own victimization – not necessarily consciously -- limits the application of his findings. In point of fact, as the field of victimology developed, his work was criticized for placing too much responsibility onto the victim for his/her injury or loss and may have contributed to the genesis of the concept of "blaming the victim." Nonetheless, he is consistently commended with being the first person to realize that the victim was a critical element within the "dialectic" nature of a criminal relationship, which did herald the start of scientific inquiry into the nature and causes of victimization.

During research into homicide patterns, Von Hentig (1948) conducted an exploration into the relationship between perpetrators and victims. His "general classes of victims" included those that he perceived to be weak, and therefore, "most likely to be a victim of an attack". Those general classes included the young, the old, females, and the mentally defective[35].

Von Hentig goes on to mention other "typical victims" which he identifies as "the immigrant, the minority race, and the 'dull normals' (pg. 414). This victim typology has a particular application to this study on many levels. Von Hentig claims that the vulnerability of the immigrant is less a function of linguistic differences and more a result of the isolation and unfamiliarity with social norms and rules. With respect to minorities, he claims that such individuals do not enjoy the same protections from the law as do the dominant class members, thereby making it easier to victimize them. And finally, a person identified as "dull" is seen as a perfect victim. They fall, intellectually, outside of the immunity extended to very old and very young by

---

[35] He went on to develop the concept "mentally defective" from birth or from an early age. He classified such "defective" individuals as either "idiots" – those unable to guard themselves against common physical dangers; "imbeciles" – those incapable of managing themselves or their affairs (or those never taught how to); "feebleminded persons" – those who require care, supervision and control for their own protection or the protection of others; and "moral imbeciles" – those with a permanent mental defect coupled with strong vicious or criminal propensities. (pg. 411-12)

"honourable thieves" (Sutherland, 1937) and are, generally, not smart enough to know they are being victimized.

Despite evidence to suggest that assaults committed against persons with disabilities are as high as ten times the general population (see Sobsey, 1991; Baladerian, 1991; Sullivan, et.al., 1987), one particular population seems to face not only disproportionate targeting for criminal victimization, but also virtually no attention in victimization literature – the Deaf. This is true even though von Hentig dedicated an entire chapter to the subject of deafness (1948:79). Unfortunately, he wrote from the perspective of Deaf offenders rather than Deaf victims. Nonetheless, much of what he attributed to the criminal behaviors of Deaf persons has equal application to Deaf victims, namely that of social isolation and cultural resentment.

Victimization Theories

The late 1970's produced studies that proved that criminal victimization did not happen randomly (Hindelang et al., 1978; Sparks, Genn & Dodd, 1977). This new realization dramatically shifted the paradigm of victimology from "wrong place, wrong time" to a new search for the factors that increased one's risk of victimization, and what emerged was examination of victims as agents in their victimization. New theories evolved that explored the role of the victim, not for purposes of affixing blame, but for the broader purpose of identifying specific risk factors and developing crime preventive strategies. A brief description of these theories and the relevance to this study are discussed below.

The belief that individuals with a propensity for criminal behavior carefully evaluate risks versus rewards and engage in some degree of target selection is firmly rooted in traditional criminal theory as the rational choice theory (Clarke & Cornish, 1985). Simply put, this perspective focuses upon the offender's decision making process (Felson and Clarke, 1998:7).

During the 1970's, traditional crime theories "explicitly rejected deterministic and pathological explanations of crime in favor of those emphasizing its purposive, rational and mundane aspects" (Clarke &

Cornish, 1985:150). As a result, research shifted its focus to the "purposive behavior designed to meet the offender's commonplace needs for such things as money, status, sex, and excitement", and particularly, how "meeting these needs involves the making of (sometimes quite rudimentary) decisions and choices..." (Clarke, 1997: 9-10). What is germane to this discussion is whether or not the Deaf community is perceived (by potential offenders, either hearing or Deaf) as one of the "socially stigmatized groups" that represent "preferred targets for different types of attacks" (Fattah,1993: 250-251).

Rational Choice Theory

If it is true that offenders choose their victims because of individual characteristics that make them attractive targets, then we must consider what those characteristics might be. For example, a person who is Deaf would not be able to hear someone approaching from behind, or would be unable to call for assistance if they were non-verbal. Such factors may contribute to a potential offender perceiving a greater chance of success were they to select a Deaf person for victimization.

The target attractiveness of a Deaf person also extends beyond the actual criminal incident. For instance, rational choice theory holds that an offender engages in a careful mental process that evaluates the risks of punishment (or getting caught) against the possibility of achieving pleasure. The complexity of thought processes varies with the challenge of the gain. If an offender perceives a Deaf person to be isolated or unable to tell someone the details of what occurred, then the risk of punishment is dramatically lowered, and the act is likely to occur – if a motivated offender were the only factor under consideration.

Further, if it is accepted that the Deaf are an insular and isolated community, then any discussion of target attractiveness must include an exploration into how the offender and victim managed to arrive at the same place at the same time. Such explanations can be found in lifestyle exposure theories, such as proximity hypothesis, equivalent group hypothesis, or routine activity theory. In general, lifestyle exposure theories posit that an individual's risk of criminal victimization depends upon his/her exposure to offender populations, and that exposure is determined by an individual's lifestyle and / or routine activity (Shaffer and Ruback, 2002).

Proximity Hypothesis

The proximity hypothesis proposes that people become crime victims simply because they happen to live or work in areas with large criminal populations. It is based more on a probability of occurrence than a statement of victim or offender behavior. It has applicability to this study in as much as it contributes to the hypothesis being tested that "The Deaf will report a higher rate of victimization from other persons who are Deaf". This idea is conceived from a logical path that if it is true that motivated offenders carefully choose easy targets, and it is true that the Deaf live close to other Deaf, then it would be very possible to argue that Deaf could victimize other Deaf.

Equivalent Group Hypothesis

Another possible explanation may be found in the equivalent group hypothesis which is a lifestyle view that argues that victims and offenders share similar characteristics because they are not actually separate groups and that in fact, a criminal lifestyle exposes people to increased levels of victimization. Recognition that an individual can transition easily between potential victim and potential offender has particular application in studies that explore how often offenders are also victims. Such an issue is not unrelated to this study and so is mentioned as a possible explanation as to why Deaf would be victimized by other Deaf, as well as something that may offer guidance for future research.

This acceptance that individuals are most likely to interact with those who are similar to themselves provides the foundation of the hypothesis to be tested in this study. That is "the Deaf will be victimized by individuals known to them" – influenced in large part from the research that suggests that an individual's victimization risk is directly proportional to the number of characteristics they share with offenders (Hindelang, Gottfredson, and Garofalo, 1978).

Traditional crime theories are criticized for being "pursued too much in isolation from each other" (Clarke and Cornish, 1985:155). This criticism, coupled with a growing recognition of the potential contributions from other disciplines (i.e.: economics, sociology, psychology, etc) has resulted in criminology expanding its previously narrow range of analysis.

By the end of the 1970's, criminology was an accepted area of scientific inquiry, but the limitations presented in the uni-dimensional characteristics of examining criminal events from only an event perspective or an offender perspective became quickly evident. Awareness of the interactional nature of crime emerged, and from that a new sociological science developed that explored criminal events for purposes of determining whether victim selection [by an offender] could be predicted based upon specific victim characteristics.

In 1979, Cohen and Felson introduced the routine activities theory, and in so doing, revolutionized and energized the field of victimology. Their theory successfully integrated the relationship between victim and offender, while simultaneously marrying that unit with opportunity – addressing both the situational (lifestyle) and temporal elements of a criminal incident. The theory, as presented, attempted to explain crime trends independent from conventional theories that focused on offender motivation (Clarke & Felson, 1993: 2).

Routine Activities Theory

The key elements of the Routine Activities Theory (Cohen & Felson, 1979) include: **suitable targets**, defined as the conditions that make a target attractive; **likely offender**[36] which refers to an individual(s) who

---

[36] "likely offender" was specific vocabulary chosen to avoid any tendency to examine "motivations". A likely offender was viewed as anyone who for any reason might commit a crime (Clarke & Felson, 2004, pg. 2)

has more to gain from the commission of the criminal act than by behaving lawfully; and "a lack of **capable guardian**" which relates basically to the absence of anything in place to protect the "suitable target". Critical to the application of this theory is the understanding that those three elements must convergence in time and space which leads to the creation of an opportunity for a criminal incident.

What makes this theory consistently attractive is that it lends itself well to explaining property crimes, but can also successfully explain intimate and violent crimes. The main criticisms are that it offers a false sense of prediction in that it seems to provide a blueprint for when a crime would occur (Clarke & Cornish, 1985:163) and it assumes a supply of motivated offenders is constant (LeBeau and Castellano, 1987). But, in fact, the criticisms have served to highlight its value in as much as this theory has successfully identified the temporal and environmental conditions ripe for a criminal event.

Most contemporary crime theories[37] now accept as true that "all persons have some probability of committing a crime and can be criminal one moment and non-criminal the next" (Clarke and Felson, 1993:10). This acceptance would seem to suggest that what remains for successful crime avoidance is to effectively identify the likely targets within a temporal framework that produces conditions conducive to criminal activity.

Although each of the theories discussed above contribute some understanding of individual criminal events; as a whole, they suggest that the "victim" had some control over changing his/her life circumstances[38] but fails to incorporate existing criminological findings regarding offender motivations and behaviors.

---

[37] See "Environmental criminology" (Brantingham & Brantingham, 1981), "hot spot" criminology (Sherman et al, 1989), "defensible space" (Newman, 1972), and "CPTED – crime prevention through environmental design" (Jeffery, 1971).
[38] "Blaming the victim" refers to attempts to assign some responsibility to the victim of a crime for the criminal act perpetrated against them.

Now, as criminology and victimology progress towards a more multi-faceted, interdisciplinary and dynamic approach to criminal incidents, it appears that virtually each emergent theory involves some unification of the basic elements included in the routine activities theory and rational choice perspective. What remains important from a policy consideration is how they differ in terms of the scope of the analysis and intended arena for change. For instance, if the examination takes place on the macro-level as suggested by the routine activities theory, then the issue is considered a societal one, and changes would have to occur within the social infrastructure; if, however, a micro-level analysis is employed, then it can be assumed that an individual is the intended target of change (suggested by the rational choice perspective). Either way, these differences point to the weaknesses of both theories and suggest that a more complete theoretical framework must exist.

Crime Opportunity Theory

Positivist explanations of crime have been largely dismissed following research that suggests that much more than simply deterministic elements contribute to a criminal incident. Classical models of crime (deterrence, free will, etc.) no longer dominate contemporary criminological theory because they do not *guarantee* a criminal event (i.e., broken homes do not always yield offenders, etc.). What does seem to fit the contemporary models of crime is the work of environmental criminologists, who have discovered that "easy or tempting opportunities entice people into criminal action" (Felson & Clarke, 1998:2). This basic principle exists in both the routine activities theory and the rational choice perspective. However, when examined together within the framework of "settings," what becomes instantly clear (and more importantly, empirically verifiable) is that more than an individual's propensity or choice to commit crime, the **opportunity** to do so more likely guarantees that an event will take place.

A new area of theoretical inquiry is evolving that rejects the static elements of traditional offender motivation theories, extends the applications of routine activity theory, and capitalizes on the contributions made by crime pattern theory. In short, focusing on the dynamic elements that contribute to the "opportunity" for crime (as a "root cause") shows more promise than earlier theories that are limited to using the individual as an explanatory element (Felson & Clark, 1998). Criminal opportunity theory[39] is based on ten main principles that include:

1. Opportunities play a role in causing all crime;
2. Crime opportunities are highly specific;
3. Crime opportunities are concentrated in time and space;
4. Crime opportunities depend on everyday movements of activity;
5. One crime produces opportunity for another;
6. Some products offer more tempting crime opportunities;
7. Social and technological changes produce new crime opportunities;
8. Crime can be prevented by reducing opportunities;
9. Reducing opportunities does not usually displace crime; and
10. Focused opportunity reduction can produce wider declines in crime.

This promising new field recognizes that situational factors, specific environments, interactions between people, and the circumstances surrounding those interactions all play a critical role in the actual occurrence of a criminal event (Felson and Clark, 1998). This approach promises a more complete explanation of criminal behaviors on both an individual and a social level. It offers cogent direction for

---

[39] These ten principles of criminal opportunity theory derive from: Felson, M. and Clarke, R.V. (1998). *Opportunity Makes the Thief: Practical Theory for Crime Prevention.* Police Research Series, #98 for the Policing and Reducing Crime Unit of the Research, Development and Statistics Directorate for the Home Office. < www.homeoffice.gov.uk/rds/prgpdfs/fprs98.pdf>

crime avoidance policies and /or procedures, and provides some guidance for the hypothesis being tested herein that "the circumstances surrounding the victimization will reflect some degree of disability exploitation". This hypothesis emanates from the assumption that if multiple factors must converge to create a criminal opportunity, then one's disability may actively function to increase one's vulnerability to assault.

Overall, it is this researcher's position that a coherent victim theory must explain individual vulnerabilities that may contribute to victimization, situational factors that explain the relationship between victim and offender, and an opportunity (or motive) for victimization. Anything less than that and the theory is incomplete, open to criticism, and would have limited applicability in the field. To meet that goal, the theoretical underpinnings of this study will include elements from the routine activities theory, the rational choice perspective and opportunity theory, and will be presented within the social structure as described in Chapter Two.

Applying Victimological Theories to Members of the Deaf Community

Uniting concepts of time, space, and opportunity with offender motivation, result in the emergence of several new variables key to explaining (and perhaps preventing) criminal incidents. The variables with specific application to the Deaf community and their risk of victimization are described below: resident location (Reiss and Roth, 1993), daily lifestyle activities (Hindelang, et. al., 1978; Lashley, 1989), demographics (Hindelang et al, 1978; Singer, 1981), personal behaviors (Smith, 1982; Hough & Mayhew, 1983; Sampson & Lauritsen, 1990) and situational elements (Fattah, 1993; Cornish, 1994).

Are persons who are Deaf seen (by potential offenders) as "preferred targets"? As pointed out by this researcher in Chapter Two, attempting to analyze crime theory, independent from the social structure in which the event takes place, will yield information with limited use in terms of policy and procedure. Whatever the findings regarding the opportunity or the motivation of offenders with respect to Deaf persons, recognition of their reality in the social hierarchy is critical to using that information in a way that will benefit both the d/Deaf and hearing communities.

The Victimization of Deaf Persons – What is Already Known

Fallahay (2000) estimated Americans with some degree of hearing loss to be 25-28 million (about 10 percent of the population). More significantly, given age demographics, that number is projected to increase significantly as the population ages, and those figures predate new information released regarding the hearing loss of the younger population due to iPods and headphones. Given the population of hearing–impaired[40] and profoundly deaf persons[41], it seems relatively safe to assume that a substantial percentage of these people will become crime victims. A critical question must then become: is the criminal justice system equipped, both physically and procedurally, to handle the challenges presented by a victim who is either hearing-impaired or Deaf? The available information suggests not.

A 1996 survey queried women with a variety of disabilities to rank the most important topics affecting their lives, 92% ranked violence as their top priority (Doe, 1997). Using that as a guide, this study focused primarily on describing and identifying specific risks for violent victimization. Since the opportunity existed, questions were also posed regarding d/Deaf rates of non-personal criminal victimization (thefts). Previous findings provided the foundation for the hypothesis that "Deaf will report generally higher levels of victimization than members of mainstream society". This concept evolved from a belief that d/Deaf

---

[40]   Data from the National Health Interview Survey, National Center for Health Statistics, Series 10, Number 188, Table 1, 1994.

[41]   Since there is no legal definition of deafness comparable to the legal definition of blindness, "deaf" and "deafness" can have a variety of meanings.

rates of victimization are dramatically underestimated based upon a series of anecdotal and official news reports.

Homicide

Cursory examination of *Deaf Today* headlines found evidence to suggest that murder is a crime perpetrated against persons who are Deaf. Table 3.1 provides some examples, which while not purported to be a complete accounting since 2002, adequately illustrate the reality of this crime as a factor in the Deaf community:

Table 3.1
Select Examples of Homicides of
Persons who are Deaf in Recent Years

Jan. 25, 2004	A deaf mute from Brooklyn, NY was fatally shot as he waited for a bus after he left a basketball game. He may not have heard his killer's demands. (003889.html)
Oct. 10, 2003	...A deaf woman, who communicated through handwritten notes, wound up fatally shot in an alley in Fort Myers, FL. (003169.html)
Jan. 17, 2003	Today police arrested a 43-year-old Randolph AFB civilian employee, on allegations he strangled his pregnant, deaf stepdaughter in December. (001233.html)
Feb. 19, 2003	A Deaf woman has been missing after leaving her three children to meet someone in Camden, NJ (The Courier Post, 2003)
Oct. 30, 2002	A 27-year-old deaf woman was found over the weekend by two loggers. She died from blunt trauma to the face and had been dead for about a month. (000301.html)
October 27, 2002	Carmen Maria Reyes, a 26-year-old deaf woman, died violently two weeks ago. (000250.html)

From www.deaftoday.com/news/archives/

Sexual Assault

Another cursory examination of *Deaf Today* headlines confirmed that sexual assault is very much a factor in the d/Deaf community:

Table 3.2
Select Examples of Sexual Assaults of Persons
who are Deaf in Recent Years

Oct. 08, 2005	A former hospice worker from Denver pleaded guilty to sexually assaulting a blind, deaf, and nearly comatose 10-year-old girl with a terminal illness. He told investigators he had sex with the girl because he wanted her to experience pleasure before she died. (2005/10/man_pleads_guil.html)
Aug. 18, 2005	A Michigan therapist used his position to lure a deaf patient into having sex. Police say he was originally charged with four counts of fourth-degree criminal sexual conduct, but will now be charged with ten more counts – five for fourth-degree criminal sexual conduct, and five for sexual penetration/unethical medical treatment of a patient by a doctor. (2005/08/therapist_accus.html)
Aug. 22, 2004	The Archdiocese of Boston suspended a Weymouth priest yesterday amid allegations he watched teenage girls undress while serving as a minister to the hearing impaired at the defunct Boston School for the Deaf. (005461.html)
Nov. 18, 2004	A judge ruled that a paroled deaf rapist accused of sexually attacking a deaf female friend, must stand trial on two counts of rape. (2004/11/deaf_parolee_to.html)
Dec. 17, 2004	A Connecticut man has been convicted of raping his former girlfriend's 13-year-old deaf daughter. Authorities claim the sexual assaults occurred in her mother's bedroom on three separate occasions. (2004/12/man_convicted_i.html)

From www.deaftoday.com/news/archines/

Empirical research on the topic of sexual abuse of deaf youth is severely lacking, in part because of the sensitive nature of the topic, and also because traditional models of research do not seem to yield results that is directed toward viable solutions to the problem (Mertens, 1996). This, despite the fact that during their lifetime, 60 percent of all hearing impaired women will become victims of sexual assault (Worthington, 1984).

There have been some pioneering attempts to produce empirical figures to quantify the problem. The findings of four such studies are:

- Sullivan, Scanlon & La Barre (1986) surveyed 322 incoming freshmen to a postsecondary educational facility. Eleven percent (37) indicated that they had been victims of sexual abuse; of those students, twenty-four also experienced physical abuse;

- Swan (1987) surveyed all incoming 9th grade students from a residential school for the deaf to determine their knowledge of sexual abuse, self-protection techniques, and their own experiences (if any) of sexual abuse. Fifty percent of the students reported that they had been sexually victimized;

- In 1987, Sullivan, et. al. conducted face-to-face interviews in ASL with 100 deaf students from 18 states receiving treatment at the Center for Abused Handicapped Children at the Boys Town National Institute for Communication Disorders in Children. Those interviews revealed home and school settings represented the areas most vulnerable to for sexual assaults; and

- Finkelhor (1986) reported that when compared to available incidence data from the general population, (1 in 10 boys; 1 in 4 girls), sexual abuse occurred at some point prior to adulthood at double the rate for d/Deaf girls (50 percent) and five times the rate for d/Deaf boys (54 percent).

Researchers have only just begun to explore the issue of sexual assault on college campuses for the hearing community (Baum & Klaus, 2005) and preliminary explorations in this area of interest have extended to the Deaf / HOH community (Joseph, et.al., 1995; Williams and White, 2001).

Domestic Violence

Attempts to locate empirical data documenting domestic violence victimization of d/Deaf women have not proven fruitful. *Deaf Today*, an online Deaf news service, reported in 2004 that more than a half-million d/Deaf women in the United States were abused (www.deaftoday.com/ news/archives/004187.html). Other sources suggest that the rates of domestic violence within the Deaf community are twice that of the national average (incestabuse.about.com/ od/domesticabuse/a/minority.htm). It is unclear where these figures originated; and therefore, they should be considered with caution. The research that does exist, however, points to a significant amount of anecdotal evidence to warrant attention to this problem. Unfortunately, anecdotes fail to effectuate the types of policy and procedural changes and long term financial commitments necessary to guarantee services to the d/Deaf community.

What is known is that research indicates that batterers often use isolation, physical violence, emotional and psychological abuse, financial exploitation, and sexual violence as part of their tactics for gaining power and control (Reyna, undated). Some authors have even suggested that "In the deaf community women will seek out an able-bodied hearing male as a partner because this is viewed as a form of status in the deaf community. In addition, able-bodied men often seek disabled women as partners. These men are looking for an imbalance of power in a relationship, which is the hallmark for abuse" (Devine & Briggs, 2001).

This report has already outlined how the Deaf community is socially isolated from the mainstream, and that isolation only increases in violent situations. For example:

- An abuser may destroy a Deaf partner's assistive communication device (TTY machine or Blackberry), essentially rendering her incapable of calling for help (Gilbride, online), or may take or destroy a victim's hearing aids or internet access, or deny them use of close-captioning on the TV;

- Domestic violence shelters may not own or know how to operate a TTY machine, resulting in virtual inaccessibility for a Deaf victim;

- Printed victim rights information or information regarding community services and resources are often prepared in English, limiting what an ASL speaking person may be able to understand.

Further, the Deaf community is extremely small and insular, and the victim who is Deaf has little chance of hiding her identity or her whereabouts if the abuser is also a member of the Deaf community, which is a distinct possibility. In the United States, at least 85% of individuals with profound deafness marry another deaf person (www.people.vcu.edu/ ~nance/marriage.html), and these numbers have remained relatively stable since 1974[42].

Since most crisis centers are ill-equipped for addressing the special needs of a victim who is Deaf, most victims choose to remain in the abusive relationship (www.ilcadv.org/legal/ special_deaf.htm#faq). A Deaf woman who knows sign language, having escaped her abusive

---

[42] In 1974, Jerome Schein and Marcus Delk reported that of the married males deafened under the age of 3: 82% had deaf spouses 7% had hard of hearing spouses; of those married males deafened between the ages of 3-18: 77% had deaf spouses 6% had hard of hearing spouses. Also, of the married Females deafened under the age of 3: 86% had deaf spouses 6% had hard of hearing spouses; and of those married females deafened between the ages of 3-18: 65% had deaf spouses 9% had hard of hearing spouses.

husband, ended up returning to him because she was uncomfortable at a shelter without devices for the hearing-impaired. "I could see the camaraderie, the friendship, and the closeness between the other women...They could speak, but I felt alone. I couldn't communicate. Groups of women would get together, talk for hours, knit blankets and make things and talk, talk, talk. But I couldn't be close" (www.deaftoday.com/news/archives/ 004968.html).

A 1997 study conducted by the Center for Research on Women with Disabilities concluded that only 22% of shelters in the United States provided abuse-related services to disabled women, and that only 5.5% offered personal-care attendant services (Nosek et.al., 2001). Recent collaborative efforts from The National Domestic Violence Hotline, the Abused Deaf Women's Advocacy Services (ADWAS) of Seattle, the National Association of the Deaf (NAD), and Deaf Women United have offered a promise of hope to Deaf victims of domestic violence. The ultimate goal of the collaboration is to unite Deaf victims, through a central Hotline, with local advocates who can facilitate communications with the various local service providers (www.ovc.gov/assist/nvaa/supp/l-ch13.htm).

What remains is a commitment from hearing professionals (DV advocates, law enforcement, medical professionals, etc.) to stop ignoring the issue of domestic violence within the Deaf community and to actively work towards overcoming communication difficulties and cultural limitations in order to equalize the services and resources available to domestic violence victims who are Deaf (www.deafhope.org/information/ powerwheel.html).

Property Offenses

No published studies examining the rates of property offenses against the d/Deaf population have been identified. While burglary alert and smoke/fire systems do exist for the Deaf/HOH community (they are assistive devices that can be connected to strobe lights, flashing lamps, or vibrating devices), the likelihood that the nature of the disability would be known in advance to a potential offender is minimal.

Therefore, it is unlikely that a victim of property crimes would necessarily be targeted because of his/her deafness.

Presumably then, a perpetrator would not be aware of the hearing status of the intended victim; therefore, there is little reason to assume that the rates of property crimes against the d/Deaf community would differ significantly from the rates against the hearing community, hence the hypothesis to be tested herein. However, given that it is possible for violent events to emerge from seemingly simple property offenses[43], the issue will be explored in this study.

The information provided above highlights the seriousness of the problem of violent victimization within the d/Deaf community and provide the foundation for the hypothesis to be tested herein that "Deaf will report a generally higher rate of victimization from violent, intimate crimes".

The Victimization of Deaf College Students – Preliminary Research

Joseph (1995) surveyed 130 Deaf or HOH college-aged students (72 % female, 28 % male) and found that approximately one-fourth were forced to have sex against their will on at least one occasion. These figures are consistent with other findings regarding the female to male ratios of sexual victimization within the hearing community. However, this study does not clarify at what age the assault is purported to have occurred, although it did determine that 52 % of the subjects initiated their sexual activity between the ages of 15 and 18 years old. Since previous studies (see Sullivan et al., 1987; Sullivan et. al., 1991; and Knutson and Sullivan, 1993) have already reported a higher risk of sexual victimization for Deaf/HOH children when compared to other

---

[43] During an attempted burglary of an apartment, two young adults assaulted the resident, who was deaf. During a court hearing, they told the judge, "The guy opened the door and... he got beat up, and things were taken." www.deaftoday.com/v3/archives/2005/01/two_more_admit.html

children either with or without disabilities, it can not be clear from this particular study that the assaults reported actually occurred on college campuses or during their college years.

Williams and White (2001) randomly administered a 121-item baseline survey to both Deaf / HOH (N = 175) and hearing (N = 779) students in an effort to measure the experiences of sexual violence among NTID/RIT college students. This survey differed from previous studies in that it surveyed only college students and limited their responses to events from "within the last school year". Table 3.3 details the findings regarding the sexual assault experiences of men and women. From that specific population, they found that nine percent of Deaf/HOH college females and nine percent of Deaf/HOH college males reported attempted intercourse against their will, and that ten percent of Deaf/HOH college males and seven percent of Deaf/HOH college females reported having intercourse against their will (Williams and White, 2001).

Table 3.3
Sexual Victimization for Deaf/HOH
By gender, for 2002

	Males (N= 99)		Females (N = 76)	
	%	N	%	N
Sexual touching against your will	22	22	22	17
Attempted sexual penetration (vaginal, anal or oral intercourse) against your will	9	9	9	7
Sexual penetration (vaginal, anal or oral intercourse) against your will	10[44]	10	7	5

(from Williams and White, 2001 – working paper)

---

[44] It is unclear at this point why the male reports of actual intercourse happening against their will is higher than female reports.

Frequency of Victimization

Some research suggests that women with disabilities are abused for longer periods of time than women without disabilities (Young, Nosek, Howland, Chapong and Rintala, 1997). Unfortunately, this study does not provide disability-specific information; it combines the figures for emotional, physical and sexual abuse; but it does not include males in the project, which severely limits the usefulness of this data other than offering the observation that women with disabilities suffer longer than women without disabilities.

For instance, while the findings are limited, they offer insight into what data would be more useful. What explanatory factors might cause the longer duration, i.e., a reduced number of escape options, severe economic dependence, the need for assistance with personal care, environmental barriers, and/or social isolation? Additionally, for the criminal justice system, it would be useful to know if *duration* referred to the length of time an individual is actually victimized, repetition of the same crime over time, as in domestic violence, or the occurrence of many different crimes within a specific time frame. Such distinctions are critical when considering the research, theory or policy implications.

Specific research into repeat and multiple victimization[45] (Outlaw, Ruback and Britt, 2002) draws heavily from the routine activity, lifestyle exposure, social disorganization (Shaw & McKay, 1942), and criminal opportunity theories to identify place-specific characteristics for victimization. Generally, research suggests that (1) areas with high rates of victimization also have high rates of repeat victimization (Trickett, Osborn, Seymour & Pease, 1992); (2) repeat victimization is determined mainly by social factors (Outlaw, et. al., 2002); and (3) multiple victimization is reported to determined more by individual characteristics than social ones (Outlaw, et al., 2002).

---

[45] Repeat victimization refers to more than one occurrence of the same type of crime within a specific time frame, whereas multiple victimization refers to many different types of crime occurring within a specific time frame.

These preliminary findings regarding the frequency of victimization for women with disabilities, and the findings surrounding the roles of individual and social level factors in the phenomenon of repeat and multiple victimizations lead to the foundation of the hypothesis to be tested in this study, that is "the deaf will have a high rate of repeated or chronic victimization".

Satisfaction with system responses to victimization

Before the Americans with Disabilities Act was passed in 1992, social service and criminal justice agencies chronically mishandled and neglected the needs of adults with disabilities who were criminally victimized. These experiences extend to the d/Deaf community and continue to result in d/Deaf victims being hesitant to access the justice system and/or social resources to assist in their recovery (Hoog, 2003).

While the United States Department of Justice is currently supporting research on the efficiency of criminal justice system responses to victims with disabilities, most experts acknowledge that these efforts are only in their preliminary stages. The result is that very little information exists as to (1) the actual rate of victimization of crime victims with disabilities; (2) existent model intervention services; and (3) appropriate criminal justice responses, such as improving reporting rates, sensitive interviewing techniques, and adaptations to facilitate victim participation (www.awol-texas.org/articles/ article8.html).

Further, what is yet to be determined is whether new policies and procedures will emerge that are disability-specific. This is an element that is critical to the successful implementation of any victim assistance or recovery plan that claims to improve system responses to victims with special needs. The "one size fits all" model will simply perpetuate the alienation and ineffectiveness of the justice and social service systems.

The above discussion provides the foundation for the hypothesis to be tested in this study that "the Deaf will report at a high rate a failure of the criminal justice system to adequately respond to their needs following victimization".

Chapter Summary

The theories and research discussed above continue to build on the foundation begun in Chapter Two, upon which the reader is led towards a fuller understanding of the need for research within this specialized population. Chapter Three moves away from the societal framework and actively works to provide an overview of contemporary victimological theories that suggest that criminal victimization is not a random occurrence but, in fact, is something that can be predicted based upon certain determinant factors.

This revelation, united with the research highlighting the extent to which Deaf citizens are criminally victimized, positions the reader to fully appreciate the need and value of this study. In as much as it may afford an opportunity for Deaf specific programs and policies -- and the funding of such, the promise of possibly preventing victimization or providing better recovery services when victimization does occur, certainly heralds a new day for the Deaf citizen.

CHAPTER FOUR

Research methodology and data

The preceding chapters have equipped the reader with the knowledge and framework necessary to analyze and evaluate the information assembled in this study. The social infrastructure has been outlined in terms of the differing realities for mainstream and marginalized populations, theoretical foundations of victimology has been explored with due respect paid to the integral relationship between traditional deterministic philosophies and emerging temporal considerations; and adequate exploration into the existence and justification for research in this arena has been presented.

What remains clear is that hearing members of society have long enjoyed the benefits of victimization research, including the development of crime prevention policies for institutions and crime avoidance recommendations for individuals. It is so far unknown whether or not similar risk factors exist within the d/Deaf[46] community since a comparable analysis of situational and environmental factors does not exist.

---

[46]   The term "d/Deaf" is used as representative of the sample population and is inclusive of culturally Deaf students and those students who prefer to employ hearing assistive devices.

Administering the Survey

What is needed is an effort to question d/Deaf persons in their language, in their environment, and respectful of their culture. That is the only way accurate, reliable information can be gathered and used to create programs specifically designed to assist d/Deaf citizens. This study used field-testing and reviewers from the Deaf subculture to ensure that the text of the document would be understood by the target population. Additionally, procedural changes were required on the first day of the survey administration to engage the respondents and ensure greater participation and more truthful responses. This is discussed in greater detail in Chapter Four.

The respondents were asked questions exploring their experience with criminal victimization from the previous twelve months (temporal marker was January 1, 2002). Only respondents 18 – 24 years old were included in the survey. The findings for this study, whenever possible, are presented in the same format as the national data samples in an effort to facilitate comparisons. The data used in this study is based entirely on the victim's self report.

Research Background

In 1994, while working on a federal crime victims grant project for the then National Victim Center[47] (Gregorie, 1994), this researcher became aware of a paucity of research and information regarding the appropriate treatment for crime victims who are disabled. In fact, the information was so limited that the handling of that section was reduced to eight basic and overly simplistic points – look the victim in the eye when speaking to her, do not stare, ask the individual how to communicate with her, etc. There was virtually no consideration for different disabilities nor any mention of how one might need to change the vocabulary, approach, or information, depending on the individual's physical, mental and/or cognitive abilities. The section fulfilled the

---

[47]   The organization is currently known as the "National Center for Victims of Crime" and is located in Washington, D.C.

federal grant requirement of acknowledging that victims could have disabilities, but did little to accommodate the individuality dictated by different disabling conditions.

Much of the earlier data collection efforts in this field focused on secondary analysis of hospital reports, social work files, etc. Few empirical efforts, if any, focused on surveying specific populations because of the obstacles presented with capturing reliable data from such a diverse group of individuals. In reality, for any research within the disabled community to provide valuable information, the survey instrument would have to be a malleable instrument capable of changing to suit the abilities of the subject, without challenging the reliability of his response. It would be an awesome and nearly impossible undertaking for anyone. So, the next best alternative is to analyze secondary data sources.

After the signing of the *Crime Victims with Disabilities Awareness Act in 1998*, organizations began to produce documents with more and more information about this otherwise overlooked field. Unfortunately, the data was not germane to the disabled community because few researchers asked them what was needed. So while the articles proliferated and the publications accelerated, little changed for the individual disabled communities. Where the problems were obvious, and the solutions more or less attainable, the victims received a considerable amount of improvement, but those communities where the information was more elusive saw little in the way of positive change.

Preliminary Phase: An Online Survey

In an effort to go directly "to the source", this researcher conducted an online data collection survey (Barrow, 1998). This survey was meant to serve as a pre-test to this project and was conducted online following published articles suggesting that the Internet affords individuals the ability to actively participate in popular culture without the stigma associated with being disabled (Balint, 2000; Hendershot, 2001). While this effort presented two main challenges -- self-selection bias and representativeness -- it was believed that the results would meet the expectation of providing "useful indicative data upon which further research may build" (Boncheck, et al., 1996). And, in fact, the data collected provided valuable information that contributed to the development of an instrument far more specific and useful to the d/Deaf community.

What became immediately clear in the on-line pre-test was the need for in-person interviewing within the d/Deaf community. This does not necessarily mean face-to-face interviewing, but the need for the d/Deaf subject to see and meet the person conducting the survey was clearly a key element in the survey being accepted by the community.

Research Design

This project seeks to gain a deeper experiential understanding for the population under investigation, and, as such, is best served by a qualitative research design. Qualitative research offers more options for data collection and is more tolerant of deviations from scientific rigors. It embraces the subjective responses of individuals and values real-life experiences and anecdotes. It adds a unique, human element while still making significant contributions to social science research (Tutty et. al, 1996). The specific methodology employed is discussed in more detail in Chapter Four.

Gaining Access to the Sample

The instant study evolved from communications with John A. Albertini, Ph.D. Department Chair, Professor, Department of Research, Rochester Institute of Technology. Dr. Albertini referred the researcher to Robert Whitehead, Ph.D., Professor, Chair of the Cooperative Research Review Committee at the Rochester Institute of Technology, National Technical Institute for the Deaf campus.

Specifically, Dr. Whitehead arranged for contact with individual Department Heads at the National Technical Institute for the Deaf to request permission to solicit individual professors for purposes of gaining access to students during class time for survey administration. From there, two department heads granted access to their professors, and nine professors then invited the researcher into the classroom and granted access to their students.

The researcher also participated in a focus group designed to better solicit and apply for grant and/or federal monies for use in setting up Deaf for Deaf assistance/recovery programs.

Sampling Method – Convenience

Often times the nature of the research question and the specificity of the target population preclude the ability to employ a random sample model. The instant study used a non-random convenience model often reserved for highly unique populations. Schroedel (1984:622) claims that data collected by convenience methods usually capture a higher proportion of socially active Deaf persons. Since qualitative research does not dictate representative samples but focuses instead on providing fertile data (Association of Qualitative Research, online), the use of a convenient sampling method is offered to be the most appropriate option. Other specific benefits offered by purposive sampling methods include:

1. Validation of a test or instrument with a known population;
2. Collection of exploratory data from an unusual population; and
3. Use in qualitative studies to study the lived experience of a specific population (Decker, 1997).

At the time that this study began, there existed no database that linked criminal victimization with disability. As mentioned above, types of disability were not considered in large scale surveys such as the census or NCVS prior to changes made in 2002[48]. The sample for this survey

---

[48]   In 1998, Congress passed the Public Law 105-301, the Crime Victims with Disabilities Awareness Act (CVDAA) which represented the first effort to systematically gather data regarding the extent of victimization among

is the first of its kind and is drawn from the hearing student population (N= 72) at Rochester Institute of Technology (RIT) and the d/Deaf student population (N=114) at the National Technical Institute for the Deaf (NTID).   Additional secondary data was collected from the National Crime Victimization Survey (NCVS) through the Bureau of Justice Statistics (BJS) website and from Gallaudet Research Institute (GRI) (2003).

The National Technical Institute for the Deaf (NTID), through the Cooperative Research Review Committee and the Rochester Institute of Technology (RIT), through the Institutional Review Board, made students available for participation under the following specific conditions: that student confidentiality would be strictly protected, identity of respondents would not be known, absolutely no attempt would be made to contact respondents after class participation, no direct communication would be made to the students unless they initiated a question, and victim assistance materials would be made available to every participant. These conditions were acceptable to the John Jay College Institutional Review Board, the Rochester Institute of Technology Institutional Review Board, and the National Technical Institute for the Deaf Cooperative Research Review Committee. Each committee accepted the study and allowed the survey to take place without restriction.

The survey was distributed to 16 classes from eight professors representing four departments.   The professors were sent a letter requesting access to their classes, and then the research team requested the participation from the individual students. Class lists were checked to make sure that no duplication would occur, and students who had taken or were taking criminal justice classes were asked not to participate.   In the end, the research project successfully captured 71 hearing students and 118 Deaf/HOH students, representing 13 % of the undergraduate enrolment from the RIT liberal arts college and 10 % of the NTID student population, respectively.

---

individuals with disabilities. The legislation required the Bureau of Justice Statistics (BJS) to enhance the National Crime Victimization Survey (NCVS) by 2000 to provide better measures of crimes against people with disabilities.

Participant Action Research (PAR)

From the outset, this researcher recognized the importance of actively involving the d/Deaf community in the research effort, of remaining flexible to making necessary changes throughout the process as guided and instructed by the participants, and of remaining loyal to the primary goal of effectuating positive social change to benefit vulnerable victims of crime. It wasn't known at the time of the survey administration, but later research revealed that those qualities were consistent with an emerging research method - - Participant Action Research (PAR).

PAR tradition criticizes the way in which power-holding elements of society are favored because they hold a monopoly on the definition and employment of knowledge (Reason, 1994:328). The d/Deaf community has long suffered from the misconception that "if deaf, also dumb". It has already been discussed that the overall educational achievements of d/Deaf persons, as judged by the social mainstream, is substandard, and that certain political ideologies existed that recognize the role that power differentials play in keeping certain members of society marginalized.

Alternatively, in PAR, the knowledge and experience of people – often oppressed groups – is directly honored and valued. It views research participants as collaborators in the identification and analysis of their own community's problems, but also recognizes the value of people with specialized training (Krogh & Lindsay, 1999). Whereas PAR researchers bring theoretical knowledge, experience, and the skills of conducting social science research, community collaborators bring practical knowledge and experience about the topics of study (Small, 1995), and the combination of both enhances the research findings.

PAR acknowledges that science cannot be neutral or completely objective in addressing social problems by emphasizing the context of the research rather than the universal laws of science (Small, 1995). In fact, concerns for the epistemology and methodology appear secondary to creating a dialogue between formally educated people and people under investigation. That dialogue is used to produce a profound understanding of the situation, and ultimately to create social change that will benefit those in the studied communities (Obinna, 2005). It is in this manner that PAR proves quite useful in studying social phenomena that have not received much previous attention.

PAR Researchers' Requirements

PAR researchers must be creative thinkers who are flexible and able to adapt quickly to changing situations throughout the research process. They must be comfortable abandoning the rigidity of traditional research methods in favor of embracing the flexibility and freedoms offered by Participant Action Research. Such freedoms include:

- using a range of methods as the social problems of interest tend to be more novel and understudied (Obinna, 2005);

- designing new instruments and techniques to gather data;

- making methodological choices about rigor (Obinna, 2005); and

- being sensitive to the needs and perspectives of their non-researcher counterparts by selecting measures that have a high degree of face validity and practical utility (Small, 1995).

Constituent Participation

The result of the on-line survey also highlighted the value of d/Deaf people participating in the design and planning phase of the project. Following the on-line survey, a second pre-test was developed, and contact was made with Pearl I. Johnson, M.A., Executive Director of the New York Society for the Deaf. Ms. Johnson invited the researcher to present the survey instrument and its goals to her social work staff at a monthly staff meeting (September, 2002) as well as to solicit their support in administering the survey to their clients. She also provided a sign language interpreter at that meeting, which was the first indication that this was a critical component in getting the information conveyed accurately to the target population. Eight respondents participated in the pre-test and their comments resulted in a complete restructuring of how the survey was administered, as well as a complete rewriting of the questions to reflect more ASL. The end result was the survey in its final form, as shown in Appendix C.

Description of the Questionnaire

The survey instrument was designed to elicit information using standard questions regarding property and violent crimes. It was generally modelled after the National Crime Victimization Survey (NCVS), but it does depart from the national model to the extent that it was intended for students who are Deaf, and, as such, may seem too bold in terms of vocabulary or may appear to have grammatical errors. However, these apparent errors are purposeful in that they are indications of how this survey differs from previous ones. It is written in the language and syntax most easily understood by persons who are Deaf – American Sign Language.

The questions posed are intentionally more specific and detailed because of the challenges presented by translating from spoken English into American Sign Language. It represents an effort to bring together many different surveys that have been successfully used in other attempts to survey differently-abled populations. For example, questions from Part II are modelled after the Competence Assessment for Standing Trial for defendants with Mental Retardation[49] and are used to measure how much of the basic vocabulary and roles within the criminal justice system the respondent is familiar with. In Part III, the questions in the sexual victimization section were from a previous study performed by Janet Duvall, M.Ed. from Ohio University – Chillicothe Campus (1998) while investigating the rates of d/Deaf adult survivors of sexual abuse. Reliance on previously tested survey

---

[49]   This is not to suggest that the d/Deaf suffer from some degree of mental retardation, but simply because the language was simple and translated well into ASL. Additionally, the questions asked very basic information about the criminal justice system and a basic familiarity was what was being tested.

instruments will improve the ability to compare the results from this survey to those of other victimization surveys.

Since the opportunity existed to maximize the collection of victimization data, the survey included questions about all index crimes, from sexual offenses to property crimes. Also, since offenses need not and often do not, occur independently of one another, it was believed that asking questions about possible property crimes would yield a richer understanding of the situational events surrounding victimization.

Finally, the vast majority of the questions are close-ended because the literature indicates that adults who are Deaf do not perform well on open-ended questionnaire formats because they write in ASL syntax.

Survey Instrument

The survey instrument was constructed following several rewrites. The final instrument is comprised of three distinct parts:

Part One: Personal Background Information

Part One includes eleven questions relating the respondents' demographics for purposes of identifying comparable groups. Generally, federal and state level victimization studies indicate that crime victimization is greatly influenced by a victim's demographic variables such as gender, race, age, and geographic location. This study attempts to determine whether or not such accepted findings apply equally to members of the d/Deaf community.

Part Two: About the Criminal Justice System

Part Two includes a fifteen question quiz to determine the respondents' basic knowledge of the criminal justice system (vocabulary, roles, personnel, etc.) for purposes of measuring the degree of involvement / disenfranchisement the d/Deaf experience with respect to their relationship to mainstream society.

It is hypothesized that if the d/Deaf community fails to understand how the criminal justice system works, involvement may become something to fear – therein something to avoid, even if they are innocent victims. Therefore, if it can be demonstrated that persons who are Deaf are significantly disenfranchised from society's social control mechanisms, then the level of mutual awareness between the d/Deaf and the criminal justice system would be impaired, thereby acting as another barrier to the ultimate goal of equal access to justice.

Part Three: Victimization

Part Three included thirteen headline questions (correlated to the index crimes) designed to elicit information regarding individual experiences with violent, sexual, intimate, and property crimes. Also questions were asked that attempted to measure one's satisfaction with the criminal justice system.

Each headline question had six sub-questions which were asked if the respondent answered "no" to the main question. This afforded the opportunity to gather information on one's lifetime likelihood[50] of victimization, provided insight into how much communication takes place within the d/Deaf community regarding exposure to crime, and provided an opportunity to infer the level of trust that exists between the community and the police.

If the respondent answered "yes" to the headline question, they were then directed to fourteen sub-questions. Sub-questions 1-4 were designed to gain specific information regarding offender-victim relationships, victim targeting, and temporal and environmental

---

[50] **Lifetime likelihood** refers to a risk factor that has been derived from a cumulative risk of victimization analyzed over a span of 60+ years. This statistic differs from **incidence rate**, which represents a calculated risk based upon the raw number of known offenses divided by a standardizing base, for example, 1,000 households or 100,000 people (Karmen, 2001:81-83).

considerations. Sub-questions 5 and 6 were designed to inquire about the level of crime reporting that takes place within the d/Deaf community and questions 7 – 14 were designed to establish a "satisfaction" type score for the criminal justice response to reported incidents.

In total, part three had 49 pages, but the format and sub-questions for each of the questions was exactly the same. So after reviewing the first two questions, the process of completing the survey proceeded quickly. Nonetheless, concern over respondent fatigue resulted in a shifting of question order from increasing violence (property offenses to sexual assault) as presented on the NCVS to decreasing violence (sexual assault to property offenses). This presented the best chance of capturing data regarding violent offenses if the respondents should stop mid-way through the survey.

Protection of the Well-being of Respondents

A key safeguard in this study was the effort on the part of the researcher to guarantee the mental and emotional well-being of the subjects while also obtaining the most reliable information possible. Those two factors are closely intertwined since the more the respondents trusted the researcher, the more likely they would be to share personal information.

To that end, several innovative measures were taken to facilitate the administration of the survey, as well as to guarantee the optimum protection to both the d/Deaf and hearing respondents' emotional and physical well-being.

Survey instrument

During the pre-testing of the instrument, it became clear that if a respondent answered "no" to the headline question, they would complete the survey in fairly short order, thereby clearly identifying those respondents who had experienced victimization because of the numerous follow-up questions if the respondent answered "yes". This problem was rectified by adding the six sub-questions to Part III following an answer of "no" to the headline question. Doing so not only afforded the researcher the opportunity to gather richer information, but it also served to equalize the time required to complete the survey.

Further, in an effort to convey that the surveys differed in some way, the surveys were presented to the respondents in five different-colored folders: red, yellow, green, purple and blue. There were no markings on the outside of the folders, and although the contents were identical, the researcher believed that the different colors would provide respondents with a perception of privacy[51]. Given the sensitive and specific nature of the questions, the researcher believed that even the smallest measures taken to safeguard privacy were valuable assets.

Additionally, participants were asked to remain seated at their individual desks until all of the surveys had been completed. At that time, the respondents were dismissed from class and deposited the surveys into a box provided near the door which prevented the researcher from knowing which survey belonged to which respondent. The requirement of having the respondents remain until all were completed represented another effort to reduce the identification of individuals answering questions in detail, thereby indicating victimization.

Since the survey was viewed as quite lengthy, any specific instructions to the respondents were in large (16 pt), blue or red colored print. For example, specific instructions such as "if yes, go to page ___"; and "Stop here" were in large (16 pt), colored print with pictures, where possible. This added feature allowed the respondents to move quickly and confidently through the instrument.

---

[51] It is important to mention that at no point did the researcher intentionally deceive the respondents by telling them that the contents differed. The use of the different colored folders was simply to convey an added sense of privacy.

Personal Safety & Emotional Well-Being of the Respondents

As has already been mentioned, the nature of sign language means that the individual will recall images, rather than words. Therefore, it was the feeling of the researcher that emotional services had to be included in the administration of the survey. To that end, the Student Services Department at NTID was contacted, and the procedures were discussed in terms of how best to address the possibility of the respondents' needs if a recalled memory triggered a trauma response. It was finally determined that to have a counsellor present at each survey administration would not be the best use of resources, so the department provided flyers outlining the services available to students, and a pamphlet was distributed as part of the consent packet for the students to retain. The students were encouraged to contact the Student Services Office if they felt any anxiety during or immediately following the administration of the survey.

Additionally, a sign language interpreter accompanied the researcher to Rochester, NY as a representative of the project. The interpreter is a member of the Deaf subculture because while she can hear, both of her parents were Deaf. Such individuals are recognized as Children of Deaf Adults (CODAs) and represent a valuable asset in as much as they are able to move freely through both the hearing and Deaf cultures. Use of a CODA provided the researcher the benefit of communicating the goals and direction of the survey, while simultaneously demonstrating cultural respect to the respondents. It is believed, based on comments from the participants, that this added element greatly enhanced the reception of the project.

Further, as a trained victim advocate, the researcher was able to monitor the respondents for any physical stress or trauma reactions, while the interpreter monitored in-class communications between the students for any sign of anxiety or stress.

In the end, the researcher and interpreter were approached by two respondents desiring to speak further about their experiences. It was conveyed to them that there were limitations regarding the ability of the team to assist them long term, and they were encouraged to seek the services that the school was offering.

Maintaining Confidentiality

Both IRB Committees granted a waiver of consent because it represented the only identifying document. Therefore, respondents were not asked to sign a consent form, as doing so would compromise their confidentiality. Rather, they were given an informational cover sheet (see Appendix B) to remove and retain for their information. The information included local and national contact information for victim service agencies, as well as Deaf-for-Deaf treatment options. It also included contact information for the researcher so that, if desired, the respondent could seek additional information at a later date.

As was observed during the pre-testing of the survey, respondents often preferred to ask each other about the meaning of certain words or phrases. Therefore, it was made clear during the administration of the survey that the survey and its content were strictly confidential, and any questions regarding the content should be posed to the research staff -- not to classmates.

While the researcher was permitted free access to the campus and most of the campus facilities, few of those opportunities were used. Given the sensitive nature of the survey questionnaire, and the reality that a college dormitory is the "home" for many of the students, respect for their privacy and comfort level was granted, and most free time was spent in the room compiling data and preparing for the next day. Observations were limited to openly public situations (i.e.: poolside banter, shopping, etc) where one's privacy was not compromised. Careful attention was made not to observe behaviors in the dining halls, study rooms, or classrooms, as those are areas where one has a greater than average expectation of privacy.

Research Hypotheses

Each hypothesis explored in this study is derived from a process of logical thought and a review of theories (from Chapter Three) regarding what factors would likely influence one's susceptibility to criminal targeting. The general approach and deductive logic to each hypothesis is presented in Table 4.1, as are references to any research that influenced the origination of the hypotheses.

Table 4.1
Table of Hypotheses to be Tested in this Study

Hypothesis	Idea Origin	Additional Sources
1: The Deaf will report generally higher levels of victimization than mainstream society	Research generally reports higher rates of victimization among disabled– given the unique language challenges, and social position of Deaf, rates are believed to be higher.	Sullivan et al, 1986 Finkelhor, 1986 Sobsey, 1994
1A: D/HOH NTID students will report higher victimization levels overall than hearing students at RIT/NTID		
1B: Deaf will report higher victimization rates from violent, person- to-person crimes	Emerging research in the area of sexual assault and domestic violence suggests that d/Deaf people are experiencing high rates of violent crimes.	Williams & White, 2001 Joseph et. al, 1995, Brookhauser, 1986
1C: Deaf will not experience higher property crime victimization	There is no reason to expect that a motivated property offender would necessarily be aware of the deafness of the victim, since target is an item.	
2: The circumstances surrounding the victimization will reflect some degree of disability	Routine activities assume too much and fail to account for other factors that may directly affect whether or not a crime	Felson & Clarke, 1998 – Criminal Opportunity Theory

Table 4.1
Table of Hypotheses to be Tested in this Study

Hypothesis	Idea Origin	Additional Sources
exploitation	takes place	
3: Deaf will be victimized by individuals known to them because of the insular nature of the Deaf community	Individuals are likely to interact with familiar / similar people to themselves; they find comfort in likenesses.	Hindelang et al, 1978 – Lifestyle Exposure Theory
3A: Deaf will report a higher rate of victimization from other persons who are Deaf	Motivated offenders often choose those close to them – d/Deaf often live close to one another.	Sampson & Lauritson, 1990 – Proximity Hypothesis
3B: Deaf will have a high rate of repeated or chronic victimizations	Research suggests that women with disabilities are victimized longer than non disabled Research also suggests that social characteristics affect repeat victimization, while individual affect multiple victimization.	Outlaw, et al, 2002 Young, Nosek et al, 1997
4: Deaf will demonstrate distrust and alienation from the criminal justice system	If d/Deaf are significantly isolated from social institutions, then logically, they are isolated from criminal justice system	Bronfenbrenner, 1977
5: Deaf will be dissatisfied with the services from the criminal justice system	If marginalized from mainstream – then so, too, from law enforcement agencies Simple procedures cited in Chapter 3 (ie:	

Table 4.1
Table of Hypotheses to be Tested in this Study

Hypothesis	Idea Origin	Additional Sources
	handcuffing & language) are biased against and insensitive to the d/Deaf	
5A: Deaf will report a failure of the criminal justice system to adequately respond to their needs following victimization	Historical experiences (lack of interpreter, handcuffing, etc) of the d/Deaf community in any dealings with law enforcement are the foundation of this hypothesis. Recent attempts by USDOJ to address these inequities are mentioned, but the research is so new, it is not yet completed.	USDOJ Washington State Coalition Against Domestic Violence Abused Deaf Women Advocacy

Data

This study used primary and secondary source data. The primary source is generated from the student body at the Rochester Institute of Technology and NTID. The secondary data sources are from the National Crime Victimization Survey and Gallaudet Research Institute (GRI).

The instrument used in this study included critical elements for determining the risk factors for d/Deaf persons, including, but not limited to, type of victimization, lifetime prevalence, time of day, type of weapon, race, age, gender, and with respect to property crimes, items taken, and value of items.

After receiving approval to proceed with the study, the researcher compiled 350 copies of the survey, hired a CODA, and made arrangements to visit the school on two separate occasions, January 20-

25 to survey the d/Deaf students, and March 27-29 to survey the hearing students. The survey was carefully constructed to protect the confidentiality and identity of the participants.

Each survey is numbered according when it was entered into the data base, and by request, must be maintained for a period of seven years following the administration of the survey. Additionally, they must be kept in a secure location, and no one other than the research staff can have access to the actual surveys.

Data Analysis Procedures

After reviewing the surveys, the information was classified and coded, and those variables that were to be used for this report were developed. The coding process accounted for the types of crimes experienced by the respondents, as well as descriptive statistics for the respondents, including individual demographics, situational variables, environmental characteristics, victim-offender relationships, and criminal justice system responses. After coding, the reported elements were entered into SPSS for analysis. Specifically, the researcher sought evidence of statistical significance between the groups, as well as indicators of effect sizes and direction.

CHAPTER FIVE
The Data and What it Reveals

The exact number of Deaf[52] citizens has proven to be an elusive figure, and therefore is virtually unknown (see http://gri.gallaudet.edu/Demograhics/deaf-US.php), resulting mainly from the fact that general or specific disability questions are not asked on major national data collection instruments, such as the census. When the government attempted to rectify this shortcoming on the 2000 Census, the method of inquiry failed to separate out those who were d/Deaf from those who were blind (Mitchell, 2004). Therefore, the only method available to discover the number of persons with disabilities in our society is to either examine records or membership lists from organizations that provide services to the target population, *i.e.*: the National Association of the Deaf (NAD); or to review the figures released in the federal government reports regarding recipients of Social Security Insurance (SSI). The most notable limitations of this method relate to inaccuracies arising from double counting individuals who access the services of more than one organization, or completely omitting individuals who remain isolated and unaware of services

---

[52] The term "d/Deaf" is used as representative of the sample population and is inclusive of culturally Deaf students and those students who prefer to employ hearing assistive devices.

available to them, or to choose not to access those services because doing so is to accept a label of "disabled".

Specific problems with measuring the d/Deaf population involve the reality that "deafness" lacks a legal definition. Deafness varies in degrees of severity measured along a continuum from hearing-impairment (tonal loss) to profound hearing loss (inability to hear anything beginning pre-linqually – approximately 3 years of age); in addition to the fact that as a disability, it is often age relative. This suggests that the numbers of individuals who are considered disabled as a result of hearing loss can fluctuate dramatically from year to year. Currently, best guess estimates suggest that 20 million people possess some degree of hearing loss, with 10% of those people manifesting severe or profound loss (NIDCD, 1989).

General Demographics

To compensate for the challenges introduced by both the inherent reality of studying this population, and those imposed by the dual IRB committees, this study focused on a specific age range of 18 – 24 years old which reflects the ages of typical undergraduates. Coincidentally, there exists significant statistical evidence to suggest that disproportionately high rates of violence are perpetrated by and against juveniles and young adults (Shaffer & Ruback, 2002). Extended policy implications include providing successful intervention programs to prevent future violent victimization and / or successfully identifying the risk factors that lead to violent offending. Preliminary research into juvenile crime suggests that victimization is itself a risk factor for offending or is correlated with some factor or process that is a risk factor. More research is needed to identify whether or not such risk factors extend into the arena of crimes against vulnerable populations.

Gender

The general representativeness of this sample was evaluated using data compiled from the National Center for Education Statistics. Table 5.1 below presents the gender demographics for the 18-24 year old national college student population. Assuming that 9,869,000[53] fairly represents the national population of 18-24 year olds enrolled in a degree granting institution in 2001, and accepting the NCES finding that since 1984 females have surpassed males in enrollment, (56% to 44% in 2001 respectively), then the following table is derived:

Table 5.1
Percent distribution of gender characteristics
of college age students

	NCES[1]	RIT Hearing	NTID Deaf/HOH
Gender			
POPULATION TOTAL	9,869,000	72	114
Male	4,352,229	44	70
Female	5,516,771	28	44
PERCENT OF TOTAL POPULATION	100	100	100
Male	44	61	61
Female	55	39	39

1. U.S. Department of Education, National Center for Education Statistics. (2005). Projection of Education Statistics to 2014. (NCES 2005-074). Table 11

It should be noted that both RIT and NTID reflect a reversal of the national female to male trend. However, it should also be noted that while not consistent with national findings, the gender differential is consistent with the RIT/NTID gender demographic at large, which was

---

[53] The population N of 9,869,000 represents the total Fall enrollment in all degree granting institutions for 2001 and is calculated by adding the following figures as presented in Table 11 of NCES Report 2005-005: 3,571,000 students age 18-19 years, 3,3606,000 students age 20-21 years and 2,932,000 students age 22-24 years.

60% male and 40% female as reported in the 2002 Annual Report (pg. 17). So, while not nationally representative, it accurately reflects the gender demographics of the RIT/NTID campus.

Race / Ethnicity

Using the population assumption of 9,869,000 from above, and the percentages of ethnic enrollment in degree granting institutions for 2001[54] from the National Center on Education Statistics, Table 5.2 was derived.

The small sample sizes from this survey presented significant challenges in determining the ethnic representativeness of this study, but there are some indicators that this sample may still be applicable. The percentages of white (non-Hispanic) nationally and for NTID were similar (70 % vs. 63 % respectively). Similarly, the national sample and the RIT sample the same for "other" ethnic groups at eight percent.

Both study samples failed to capture a representative population of Hispanics. However, the figures reported are consistent with overall Hispanic population at RIT which is reported in the 2002 Annual Report at a mere three percent[55].

---

[54]   U.S. Department of Education, National Center for Education Statistics. (2005). *Digest of Education of Statistics, 2004* (NCES 2006-005) Table 206. (nces.ed.gov/fastfacts/display.asp?id+98)

[55]   www.rit.edu/~wwwits/services/irps/data/data/ethnic/ethnic01.html.

.

Table 5.2
Percent distribution of ethnic characteristics
of college age students

	NCES	RIT Hearing	NTID Deaf/HOH
Ethnicity			
POPULATION TOTAL	9,869,000	72	114
White (non-Hispanic)	6,622,000	61	70
Black	1,174,000	3	14
Other[1]	740,000	6	24
Hispanic	987,000	1	4
Missing / Not Included	346,000[2]	1	2
PERCENT OF TOTAL POPULATION	**100**	**100**	**100**
White	70[2]	86	63
Black	12	4	13
Other[1]	8	8	21
Hispanic	10	1	4

1. Includes Asians, Native Hawaiians, Pacific Islanders, American Indians, or multiply ethnic.
2. 346,000 (or 3.5%) of this population are represented by nonresident aliens but are not included in the NCES figures because they were not identified in the RIT or NTID samples.

Demographic findings specific to the target population

Table 5.3 presents the comparison between the study's d/Deaf sample and data collected and reported by the Gallaudet Research Institute (GRI) regionally and nationally. GRI's data includes a regional and national student sample in which the researcher has controlled for age[56], gender, ethnicity, degree of hearing loss, and other disabling

---

[56] While the sample study is controlling for the 18-24 year old age group, GRI's 18+ sample are not necessarily college-age individuals. They are

conditions that were included on the study survey (Hotto, 2004). See Appendix A for full table.

Table 5.3
Demographic Comparisons between NTID student sample and
GRI regional and national d/Deaf samples

	NTID Student Sample		GRI Northeast Region		GRI National Sample	
AGE	**N**	**%**	**N**	**%**	**N**	**%**
Total Students Age 18-24	114	100	688	100	4108	100
Information not Reported	0	0	0	0	0	0
Total Known Information	114	100	688	100	4108	100
SEX	**N**	**%**	**N**	**%**	**N**	**%**
Total Students	114	100	688	100	4108	100
Information not Reported	0	0	3	1	25	1
Total Known Information	114	100	685	99	4083	99
Total Known Information	114	100	685	100	4083	100
Male	70	61	373	54	2259	55
Female	44	39	312	46	1824	45
RACE/ETHNICITY	**N**	**%**	**N**	**%**	**N**	**%**
Total Students	114	100	688	100	4108	100
Information not Reported	2	2	10	2	54	1
Total Known Information	112	98	678	98	4054	99

individuals who, as a function of being identified as "disabled" are able to access educational services for the disabled for an extended period of time, for instance Michigan (allows to age 26). Conversations with GRI (Hotto, Sept. 20, 2004) revealed that the individuals for their survey, while 18 years and older, were not from a college environment. Many states provide extended social or educational services to individuals with disabilities.

Table 5.3
Demographic Comparisons between NTID student sample and
GRI regional and national d/Deaf samples

	NTID Student Sample		GRI Northeast Region		GRI National Sample	
Total Known Information	112	10	678	100	4054	100
White	70	63	317	47	1967	49
Black/African Amer.	14	13	136	20	828	20
Hispanic	4	4	154	23	843	20
American Indian	0	0	0	0	47	1
Asian/Pacific Islander	16	14	37	3	245	6
Other	4	4	24	4	74	2
Multi-ethnic	4	4	10	2	50	1
DEGREE HEARING LOSS	**N**	**%**	**N**	**%**	**N**	**%**
Total Students	114	100	688	100	4108	100
Information not Reported	0	0	94	14	451	11
Total Known Information	114	100	594	86	3657	89
Total Known Information	114	100	594	100	3657	100
Hard of Hearing*	29	25	126	21	1085	30
Deaf**	85	75	468	79	2572	70
ADD'L CONDITIONS	**N**	**%**	**N**	**%**	**N**	**%**
Total Students	114	100	688	100	4108	100
Information not Reported	0	0	103	15	558	14
Total Known Information	114	100	585	85	3550	86
Total Known Information	114	100	585	100	3550	100
No additional condition	79	69	268	46	1670	47
Low Vision / Blindness	11	10	32	6	176	5
Learning disabled	10	9	115	20	503	14
Mentally retarded			105	18	733	21
Attention deficit disorder	2	2	34	6	178	5
Emotional disorder	14	12	19	3	77	2

Table 5.3
Demographic Comparisons between NTID student sample and
GRI regional and national d/Deaf samples

	NTID Student Sample		GRI Northeast Region		GRI National Sample	
Schizophrenia/Depression'	8	7				
Cerebral palsy	4	4	35	6	223	6
Other condition	4	4	61	10	430	12

  *   Whereas GRI used medical classifications to determine the "Degree of Hearing Loss", this study simply asked whether the student was "hard of Medically, the figures from the GRI Summary are inclusive of all classifications 41-55 dB and below hearing" or "Deaf".

  **   Medically, the figures from the GRI Summary are inclusive of all classifications 56-70 dB and above.

Gender / Race

Gender differences although slightly greater in this sample than for the regional or national samples, were consistent with the gender differences at NTID for 2002 (56 % male, 44 % female), as well as for the general college campus (RIT) which had a student population made up of 61 % male and 39 % female students in 2001.

As expected, the study captured a disproportionate percentage of whites (63 %) which was significantly higher than GRI's regional and national figures. However, once again, the instant sample was different, in that it is limited to a college campus rather than a broad social or educational program servicing individuals who are d/Deaf over the age of 18. This fact may also explain why the regional and national samples captured a greater percentage of African American and Hispanic persons. Finally, RIT's active recruiting efforts towards students seeking an engineering or technology concentration may explain why this study captured such a large percentage of Asian/Pacific Island students.

Auditory Ability

Participants were asked to identify themselves as d/Deaf or Hard of Hearing (HOH). Of the 118 NTID students who completed the survey, 87 students (74 %) identified themselves as d/Deaf and 31 (26 %) as Hard of Hearing. Since "deafness" does not have a legal definition, the classification of one as being d/Deaf is defined by other d/Deaf as an individual who uses ASL as their primary language, who participates in Deaf subculture and knows what is included in Deaf subculture in terms of the social values, social norms, history, traditions, and identity.

Additional Disabling Conditions

The study participants were asked to self-identify any additional disabling conditions that they may have, but it was not required nor requested that those conditions be medically diagnosed, (*see Appendix C for the wording of question # 11 in Part 1 of the survey*). Please note that this may cause some data to differ significantly from the regional and national comparative sample, and represents an area of improvement if the study is performed again.

Participants were queried regarding additional disabling conditions because such information is necessary to evaluate whether or not they were chosen for victimization as a function of their deafness, or some other, perhaps more visible, disability. Of the number of students who answered the question, 69 % of the students reported deafness being their only disabling condition. This figure was higher than the GRI samples; however, the GRI samples had a stricter medical definition for deafness, whereas the study sample included those who were hard of hearing, as well. Survey respondents indicated that they suffered from limited vision at ten percent, which was also higher than the GRI sample. However, onece again, the GRI relied on a medical classification, whereas this sample simply inquired about whether the individual had vision trouble. The higher percentage seems to suggest that more students perceive themselves as having a vision problem, especially if they wear glasses.

With respect to learning disabilities, the study sample reported a very low rate (9 %) of learning disability, as opposed to the regional (20 %) and national (14 %) GRI samples. Initially, these differences resulted from the fact that the GRI samples are not limited to a college population, and therefore, are more likely to capture higher populations. However, two additional possibilities exist to explain this difference. First, d/Deaf students have historically been considered by mainstream educators to be learning disabled, and it may be that since this question relies on self-perceptions, the students are choosing not to identify themselves as having a learning disability. Second, 12 % of the study population reported having emotional disorders (as opposed to only three percent of GRI Regional and two percent of GRI National). This disorder was described to the students as "having trouble thinking about things". It may be that the students have mislabeled their disorders, and that some students who claim to have an emotional disorder, may, in fact, be describing a learning disorder. This situation would also explain the disproportionately lower rates of emotional disorders reported by the student population. Clearly, this presents an area for improvement for future replication.

The GRI study did not question students about depression or schizophrenia. The study sample found, however, that seven percent of the students reported some depression (one student reported schizophrenia). John Greden, M.D.,[57] executive director of the University of Michigan Depression Center, reports that "Depression is a huge problem in the college student population…and estimates that up to 15 % of the college student population may be struggling with depressive illnesses". This information is necessary as depression often follows a traumatic event, and insight may provide vital information pertaining the recovery and restoration of an individual following a criminal incident.

Some students provided information regarding "other" conditions; some examples include fibromyalgia or excema. This NTID study sample reported four percent additional conditions, as compared to 10

---

[57]   Gavin, K., 2003 - www.med.umich.edu/opm/newspage/2003/college depression.htm.

% GRI regional, and 12 % GRI national, respectively. But again, the GRI samples were much larger and were not limited to the college population.

Levels of active participation in Deaf subculture

Inclusion in d/Deaf subculture involves the use of American Sign Language (ASL) as a preferred means of communication. It is accepted as a cultural unifier, since it was developed "by d/Deaf for d/Deaf". Therefore, after determining whether the subject was d/Deaf or Hard of Hearing, this study asked a secondary question of "If deaf, are you Oral or ASL?"

Table 5.4 reports that only 95 students (80 %) answered this question, of those 57 (60 %) identified themselves as using ASL exclusively, while an additional eight students (8 %) use ASL in combination with oral methods of communication (speaking, lipreading, etc), and the remaining 30 students (32%) prefer oral communication methods.

This distinction is important in as much as it may impact the degree of acceptance by other d/Deaf. Also of interest is the high percentage of HOH students who chose not to answer the question, 65% (N = 20). This may be because these questions were designed to elicit participation levels in Deaf subculture. Presumably, individuals who are HOH are able to actively participate in both hearing and deaf worlds, and therefore, do not feel a need to engage fully in the Deaf subculture.

HARPER COLLEGE LIBRARY
PALATINE, ILLINOIS 60067

Table 5.4
Preferred communication method as a cultural identifier

	Are you oral, use ASL or both?			
	Oral	ASL	Both	Total
Deaf	23	54	7	84
Hard of Hearing	7	3	1	11
Total	30	57	8	95*

* 23 students chose not to answer the question

A second key component to the d/Deaf cultural experience is the residential school environment. This is believed to be where most, if not all, of the history, tradition, and pride of being Deaf is conveyed to younger members of the community. It is presumable then that individuals who wish to participate in Deaf subculture would seek out such an environment and may explain why (70%) of the respondents identified themselves as active members of the Deaf subculture. Table 5.5 shows that 73 % of d/Deaf actively participate in Deaf subculture, as do 62 % of the hard of hearing population. These relatively high participation rates are likely because of campus activities that foster and encourage Deaf cultural expression, i.e.: plays, concerts, clubs, etc.

Table 5.5
Participation in Deaf Culture

	Are you a member of Deaf culture?		
	Yes	No	Total
Deaf	63	23	86
Hard of Hearing	18	11	29
Total	81	34	115*

* three students chose not to answer

Hypotheses testing and findings

Table 5.6 is adapted from the Table of Hypotheses presented in Chapter Four. The remainder of the chapter is guided by the order of the hypotheses presented below.

Table 5.6
Research table of findings

Research Hypothesis	Summary of Findings & Predicted Direction	Interpretation and Action
1: The Deaf will report generally higher levels of victimization than mainstream society	The Deaf/HOH sample is too small to make valid comparisons with the mainstream sample derived from the NCVS, 18-24 year old college student population D > H	The sample size was to small for making valid comparisons between the groups. This hypothesis is not able to be tested.
1A: D/HOH NTID students will report higher rates of victimization than hearing RIT students	The Deaf/HOH students reported being disproportionately targeted for victimization for 10 of the 13 crimes queried. D > H	Observed differences for sexual and violent offenses were significant at the .05 and .01 levels, respectively, indicating a difference between the two groups; so the H_o was rejected in favor of the alternative.
1B: D/HOH NTID students will report higher rates of victimization from violent, person-to-person crimes than hearing	The D/HOH students reported being targeted for sexual crimes at a rate at least twice that of hearing students. Additionally, hearing students experienced no victimization from	With respect to five sexual offenses examined in this study (showing movies, sexual touching, sexual rubbing, fellatio and rape), observed differences between the groups appeared only with respect to sexual rubbing. The

Table 5.6
Research table of findings

Research Hypothesis	Summary of Findings & Predicted Direction	Interpretation and Action
RIT students	robbery and aggravated assault, as opposed to 10% and 5 % (respectively) of the D/HOH students. Finally, D/HOH students were targeted for simple assault at almost 5 times the rate of hearing students. D > H	differences were significant at the .05 level. However, the p-values of both fellatio and rape suggested the possibility of a trend developing – larger sample sizes are needed before this can be confirmed. In the end, H_o was rejected for sexual rubbing in favor of the H_a suggesting that the alternative hypothesis *may* be true. In person-to-person violent crimes, both robbery and simple assault were significant at the .05 level, so the H_o was rejected which allows for the possibility that the alternative hypothesis *may* be true.
1C: D/HOH NTID students will not experience property crime victimization more than the hearing RIT students	Hearing RIT students were targeted more often for 3 of the 5 property crimes explored, with one of the remaining 2 crimes representing a crime of opportunity more than targeting.	With respect to property crimes, the Deaf/HOH did not appear to be targeted more or less than the hearing students, which is consistent with the research hypothesis. None of the five property

Table 5.6
Research table of findings

Research Hypothesis	Summary of Findings & Predicted Direction	Interpretation and Action
	$D = H$	crimes examined were significant at the .05 level, so the H_o was accepted indicating no difference between the two groups.
2: Circumstances surrounding the victimization will reflect some degree of disability exploitation	Identification of "home" and "friend's house" as the locations most vulnerable to sexual assault victims indicate a degree of intimacy that suggests the offender selected their victim. However, the variables examined with respect to violent, person-to-person crimes indicate that the offenses were more determined by opportunity than by selection. $D > H$	The findings support the research hypothesis with respect to the lesser intrusive sexual offenses, indicating that the offender had a relationship with the victim, and therefore, was aware of the deafness. Since the majority of assaults took place in the home or at a friend's house, it is believed that the deafness was a factor in target selection. However, as the severity of the sexual offense increases, the indicators suggest more opportunity offending rather than target selection. With violent offenses, the reported data didn't support the research hypothesis. The incidences appear to be from opportunity, ongoing relationship (i.e., DV), or random events.

Table 5.6
Research table of findings

Research Hypothesis	Summary of Findings & Predicted Direction	Interpretation and Action
3: The d/Deaf will be victimized by individuals known to them more often than hearing because of the insular nature of the d/Deaf community	Within the d/Deaf student population, 60% of sexual victims; 47% of personal, violent victims; and 44% of property crime victims identified their offender. When compared to similar findings from hearing students, 62% of sexual victims; 33% of personal, violent victims; and 10% of respondents of property crime victims identified their offender. Overall, hearing students reported less victimization by individuals they knew than d/Deaf students. D > H	The reported data shows that in sexual and violent offenses, more Deaf students knew their offenders than hearing students. With respect to property crimes, the majority of both populations under investigation did not know their offenders. Since the property crime finding is not unexpected given that most property crimes occur in the absence of a victim, the data supports the research hypothesis.
3A: The Deaf will report a higher rate of victimization from other persons who are Deaf	Of the 144 total criminal incidents described by d/Deaf respondents, only 103 incidents had answers regarding the hearing status of the offender. Since this line of inquiry was so	Analysis of each of the three crime categories consistently indicates that the Deaf are victimized more often by hearing persons than by Deaf persons. This finding is contrary to the research

Table 5.6
Research table of findings

Research Hypothesis	Summary of Findings & Predicted Direction	Interpretation and Action
	sensitive, it is unclear as to whether or not these findings can be relied upon, and therefore, the researcher cannot accept nor reject the null. . D > H	hypothesis and may be indicative of a cultural taboo against inter-group assault. At this time the findings are inconclusive - although preliminary investigation appears to support the hypothesis. Further work is necessary in this area
3D: The Deaf will have a high rate of repeated or chronic victimizations	Overall, 44 % of d/Deaf students reported repeat or chronic victimization, as opposed to only 35 % of hearing students. Further analysis explored whether d/Deaf or hearing students faced a greater vulnerability to repeat or chronic victimization for a particular type of crime, and the findings suggest that d/Deaf students faced a particular vulnerability to sexual and violent crimes. D > H	The data supports the research hypothesis that the d/Deaf were chronically victimized more than the hearing: sexual, 41% D vs. 33% H; violent 44% D vs. 0% H; and property crimes 35% D vs. 37% H. However, it should be noted that with respect to the rates of repeat assault, the Deaf were more likely to experience singular events: Sexual: 59% S vs. 41% M Violent: 55% S vs. 44% M Property: 65% S vs 35% M Where S = singular event; M = multiple event.

Table 5.6
Research table of findings

Research Hypothesis	Summary of Findings & Predicted Direction	Interpretation and Action
4: The Deaf will demonstrate significant disenfranchisement from the criminal justice system	This project examined the depth of Deaf/HOH involvement with mainstream culture. This was achieved by devising a basic quiz (derived from the CAST-MR) that measures the level of knowledge Deaf/HOH have with the criminal justice system. D > H	d/Deaf students had an average score of 56, compared to the average for hearing students of 79. This appears to confirm that society is more successful at educating hearing citizens in issues critical to mainstream culture, specifically those regarding the basic services and functions of the criminal justice system. Specific areas challenging for the d/Deaf included (1) procedures employed in the resolution of a case, i.e., plea bargaining or conviction, (2) the specific roles and responsibilities of the criminal justice system personnel, and (3) the professional responsibilities of courtroom personnel, i.e., prosecutor and judge. Further analysis revealed not only a higher average grade for hearing than for Deaf, but also statistical differences between the

Table 5.6
Research table of findings

Research Hypothesis	Summary of Findings & Predicted Direction	Interpretation and Action
		groups for 13/15 questions. The observed differences between the hearing and Deaf were mostly at the .01 level. Therefore, the H_o was rejected suggesting that the alternative *may* be true.
5: The Deaf will be dissatisfied with the services from the criminal justice system	Students identified 194 people that they told of their victimization; only 27 were the police. D < H	Low reporting rate, with the highly unlikely fact that a criminal act could occur, be investigated, prosecuted, and adjudicated in just one year results in the determination that the data for this hypothesis is inconclusive.
5A: The Deaf will report a failure of the criminal justice system to adequately respond to their needs following victimization	A low reporting rate interferes with the ability of the criminal justice system to respond. Also, the survey didn't ask about what, if any, services were made available to d/Deaf victims. So the collected data is inadequate to measure this hypothesis. D < H	The unlikely occurrence of case resolution within the short time frame of just 13 months, this research hypothesis also could not be tested, and the findings are inconclusive.

NB: D = Deaf; H = Hearing

Overall victimization of NTID students compared to mainstream society

In 2005, the Bureau of Justice Statistics published the *Violent Victimization of College Students, 1995-2002* (Baum & Klaus, 2005) which has unique and direct implications for this study. Table 5.7 presents the data regarding mainstream society's rates of victimization as reported for the 18-24 year old college student population but is limited to violent crimes, while Table 5.8 attempts to use the findings from this study to show similar data from the d/Deaf student population.

Table 5.7
Rates of Criminal Victimization from 2002
Hearing College Students, Age 18-24 years

Students (18-24 y)	Population N	Rape / Sexual Assault	Robbery	Simple Assault	Agg. Assault
Mainstream[1]	7,894,930	4	5	38	14
Gender					
Male	3,796,380	1	7	50	21
Female	4,098,550	6	3	28	6

*   Rates presented are per 1,000 persons

1   Data collected from the Bureau of Justice Statistics Special Report (NCJ206836) *Violent Victimization of College Students, 1995-2002* and reflect an average over 7 years.

Given the vast discrepancies in sample sizes, it is impossible to make valid comparisons between mainstream society (Table 5.7) and the d/Deaf sample groups (Table 5.8). Since the sample Deaf/HOH population is quite small and a larger size could effect different results, and since the national sample is not geographically restricted and the rates could differ if the figures were controlled for the Northeast region, the researcher determines that the hypothesis being tested that the persons who are Deaf will be generally victimized more than mainstream society is as yet unsupported.

Table 5.8
Rates of Criminal Victimization for 2002
for NTID Deaf/HOH Students, Age 18-24 years

Students (18-24 y)	Population N	Rape/ Sexual Assault	Robbery	Simple Assault	Agg. Assault
Deaf/HOH	118	67	101	59	119
Gender					
Male	73	41	123	55	109
Female	45	111	67	67	133

** Rates presented are per 1000 persons

It is possible, however, to examine some within-group similarities. For instance, simple assault was the highest reported crime for both groups suggesting that both mainstream college students and college students who are Deaf often find themselves in altercations without weapons, possibly resulting in some type of minor injury.

Also within both groups, African Americans more often reported being targeted for crimes of aggravated assault. This suggests that whether or not injury actually occurred, a weapon was involved. Such a factor increases the risk of fatal injury and can contribute to the rapid escalation of confrontation – particularly if one of the parties is not clearly understood, as is the case with a victim who is Deaf.

Within both groups, males were more often targeted than females for crimes of robbery, aggravated assault, and simple assault, whereas the females experienced greater targeting for sexual crimes. Interestingly, the rates of sexual crimes differed significantly between the mainstream male population, and the d/Deaf male population which is consistent with current literature regarding the sexual crimes against the Deaf community (see Finkelhor, et.al., 1990; Senn, 1988 and Sullivan, et.al., 1987), in as much as the findings suggest rates almost as high for d/Deaf males as for d/Deaf females. The gender rate difference for the mainstream group was five percent, whereas the difference in rates for the d/Deaf gender group was a mere one percent.

Overall victimization of NTID students at NTID compared to RIT students

The data presented in Table 5.9 reflects responses to question 6 in Part I – Demographics: "Have you been a victim of crime since January 2002?" It was asked in order to orient the reader to the time frame and prepare them for the general content of the survey. The figures reported in Table 5.9 suggest that the reported data does not support the hypothesis that Deaf/HOH students will report higher levels of victimization than hearing students at RIT/NTID.

Table 5.9
Rates of Criminal Victimization since January 2002
for Deaf/Hard of Hearing and Hearing Students

	Deaf (N)	Hearing (N)
Have you been a victim since January 2002?		
Yes	10	9
No	97	52
Miscellaneous*	8	10
Won't Tell	3	0
Total	118	71
Percent Total	100	100

* Have combined "Don't Know" and "Can't Remember"

However, when those responses were analyzed for accuracy (based on what was reported in Part III, where respondents were provided a specific example of what constituted a crime), the findings were significantly different. Of the 52 hearing students who reported no victimization during 2002, 15 (29 %) of those students provided specific details of victimization that took place during the past year in Part III. Likewise, of the 97 Deaf/HOH students who claimed no victimization during 2002, 52 (54 %) went on to provide specific details in Part III about victimization that took place over the past year.

The Omnibus Test of Model Coefficients showed a chi-square value of 32.047 (df = 13) for the whole model, which indicates that the model is significant at the alpha 0.05 level (df: 13, x^2 = 22.3621). This finding affords the researcher the opportunity to pursue further statistical explorations to determine the degree to which it can be empirically reported that the d/Deaf are being targeted more often than their hearing counterparts for criminal victimization.

Table 5.10
Chi-Square Tests of Significance for Criminal Categories

Criminal Offense	Directional tendency $N= 189$	Df	X^2 value	p value
Sexual Offenses [1]	D (78%) > H (22%)	1	4.044*	.044
Violent Offenses [2]	D (91%) > H (9%)	1	13.053**	.000
Property Offenses[3]	D (67%) > H (33%)	1	0.737	.391

D = d/Deaf students; H = Hearing students

* = significant at the 0.05 level; ** = significant a the 0.01 level

1= inclusive of (1) forced to watch movies; (2) sexual touching w/out permission; (3) sexual rubbing w/out permission; (4) fellatio and (5) rape.

2= inclusive of (1) robbery; (2) simple assault and (3) aggravated assault.

3= inclusive of (1) personal theft; (2) burglary; (3) property theft; (4) motor vehicle theft and (5) forgery.

The findings in Table 5.10 indicate an observed difference to a statistical significance with respect to sexual and violent offenses, indicating that the null hypothesis should be rejected in favor of the alternative hypothesis. The findings also indicate no observed difference in property crimes between the two groups dictating that the null hypothesis should be accepted.

Therefore, it appears that the data supports the research hypothesis that Deaf students will report generally higher levels of criminal victimization than hearing students at RIT/NTID.

Violent victimization of d/Deaf NTID students compared to RIT students

Since Table 5.10 determined that the Deaf do face increased vulnerability to sexual and violent offenses to a statistical certainty, further analysis was conducted to determine which of the individual crimes contributed to the size and direction of the effect. Those findings are presented in Table 5.11.

Table 5.11 examines the directional tendency for each violent criminal event, reports the chi-square finding for each offense at the 0.05 level with one degree of freedom and provides the *p*-value. The data indicates that d/Deaf students report higher rates of victimization for every sexual and violent crime investigated in this study.

Table 5.11:
Chi Square Tests of Significance for Individual Criminal Events

Criminal Offense	Directional tendency N= 189	df	X² value	p value
Showing movies	D (80%) > H (20%)	1	0.67569	.411
Sexual touching	D (74%) > H (26%)	1	1.47125	.225
Sexual rubbing	**D (100%) > H (0%)**	**1**	**5.68602***	**.017**
Fellatio	D (100%) > H (0%)	1	3.09023	.079
Rape/Penetration	D (89%) > H (11%)	1	2.81989	.093
Robbery	**D (100%) > H (0%)**	**1**	**7.70985***	**.005**
Simple Assault	**D (88%) > H (12%)**	**1**	**4.68267***	**.030**
Aggr Assault	D (87%) > H (13%)	1	2.23785	.135

D = d/Deaf students; H = Hearing students

* = significant at the 0.05 level; ** = significant at the 0.01 level

Statistical analysis revealed that the criminal offenses revealing the greatest significant differences were sexual rubbing without permission, robbery, and simple assault. Additionally, while not statistically significant, the *p*-values for fellatio and rape, 0.079 and

0.093 respectively, indicate a trend in the data. Further analysis and larger sample sizes are required before any definitive relationship between the groups can be determined.

A corollary inquiry is how the figures reported in this survey compare to those reported by the RIT to the Office of Postsecondary Education, in accordance with the Clery Act guidelines. In general, the figures reported by RIT are dramatically lower than those reported herein. To a certain extent, that is not surprising since victim surveys consistently reflect higher crime rates than official records, as they are more apt to capture the "dark figures of crime". Still, even considering the established disconnect for crime reporting, RIT's figures are very low. Further, RIT reports its figures as one campus, so it is virtually impossible to determine which of RIT's eight colleges has the greatest vulnerability. Keeping this in mind, Table 5.12 reports the rates for the 2002 school year as:

Table 5.12:
Campus Security Statistics
For Rochester Institute of Technology, 2002

Crime	On Campus	Residence Hall	Total
Rape	0	9	9
Robbery	0	0	0
Aggr Assault	0	1	1
Burglary	12	61	73
Vehicle Theft	6	1	7

Data collected from the U.S. Department of Education, Office of Postsecondary Education (OPE) Campus Security Statistics website, <retrieved on 10/22/2006>

As mentioned above, d/Deaf students reported higher rates of victimization for every violent crime explored. What follows below is an examination of the two criminal categories inclusive of violent crimes: sexually based offenses and violent intimate offenses.

Sexually-based Offenses

It has been reported that "not only are the rates [*of sexual abuse*] for the deaf children much higher, but the sex ratio is reversed, *i.e.,* among the deaf, more boys than girls experience abuse (Sullivan, et. al., 1987). Table 5.12 shows that this report did not replicate those findings. In fact, the ratio of sexual assault between the genders was the same for both hearing and Deaf student populations, namely that females were assaulted consistently at twice the rate of males. However, within the individual populations, the observed difference between Deaf males and Deaf females proved to be statistically significant for sexually based offenses.

Table 5.13
Chi-Square Tests of Significance for
Sexual Crimes, Hearing status by gender

Sexually-based offenses	Directional tendency N= 189	df	X² value	p value
Deaf/HOH	**F (31%) > M (15%)**	1	**4.291***	.038
Hearing	F (14%) > M (7%)	1	1.019	.313

F = female; M = Male
* = significant at the 0.05 level

Since Table 5.13 determined that there is a significant difference between the sexual victimization of d/Deaf females and d/Deaf males, further analysis was conducted to determine which of the individual sexually-based crimes contributed to the size and direction of the effect. Those findings are presented in Table 5.14, which presents the directional tendency for each sexually-based crime investigated, reports the chi-square finding for each offense at the 0.05 level with one degree of freedom, and provides the *p*-value.

Table 5.14
Chi-Square Tests of Significance for Sexual Crimes
Deaf/HOH students, by gender

Sexually-based offenses	Directional tendency $N= 189$	df	X^2 value	p value
Movies	F (4%) > M (3%)	1	.247	.619
Touching	**F (24%) > M (8%)**	**1**	**5.943***	**.015**
Rubbing	F (11%) > M (6%)	1	1.253	.263
Fellatio	F (4%) = M (4%)	1	.008	.930
Rape	F (11%) > M (4%)	1	2.159	.142

F = female; M = Male
* = significant at the 0.05 level

The data indicates that d/Deaf females report higher rates of victimization for every sexual crime investigated in this study except for fellatio, where those rates of assault are equal for the genders. It also indicates that the only sexual offense that shows a statistically significant finding is sexual touching without permission.

Violent, Intimate Offenses

Table 5.15 shows that this report did not find a significant difference between the d/Deaf and hearing students with respect to violent offenses. What was determined was that within the hearing community, females were more likely to be victims of violence as opposed to the d/Deaf student population, where the males are more likely to be victims of violence.

Table 5.15
Chi-Square Tests of Significance
Violent Crimes, Hearing status by gender

Sexually-based offenses	Directional tendency $N= 189$	df	X^2 value	p value
Deaf/HOH	F (20%) < M (27%)	1	.822	..365
Hearing	F (7%) > M (2%)	1	.972	.324

F = female; M = Male

Property crime victimization for NTID students compared to RIT students

Table 5.10 indicated that the Deaf do not face increased vulnerability to property offenses to a statistical certainty. Further analysis was conducted to clarify the effect size and direction for each of the property crimes examined. Table 5.16 shows that d/Deaf students report higher rates of victimization for every property crime investigated herein, except motor vehicle theft.

Table 5.16:
Chi Square Tests of Significance
Individual Property Criminal Events

Criminal Offense	Directional tendency $N= 189$	df	X^2 value	p value
Personal Theft	D (62%) > H (38%)	1	0.01013	.920
Burglary	D (76%) > H (14%)	1	2.32485	.127
Property Theft	D (70%) > H (30%)	1	0.27102	.603
Vehicle Theft	D (33%) < H (67%)	1	1.08342	.298
Forgery	D (75%) > H (25%)	1	0.28339	.594

D = d/Deaf students; H = Hearing students

* = significant at the 0.05 level; ** = significant at the 0.01 level

The rate differences between the populations could be explained perhaps by the types of transportable personal items (i.e.: iPod, laptop, wallet, etc) carried by the different populations, or by the small sample sizes. Regardless, there is no reason to suspect that differential targeting is present between the sample populations. Property theft and home burglary are often crimes of opportunity rather than specific targeting, and the opportunity model is consistent with the nature of dorm/college living arrangements.

The absence car theft crimes in the Deaf/HOH population is not surprising because college restrictions for on-campus vehicles and/or insurance premiums placed upon young drivers may make maintaining a vehicle on-campus cost prohibitive. Likewise, the higher rate of check forgery among students who are Deaf may be a result of the distribution of social security checks from the government which tend to arrive on a scheduled date, making it easier for someone to plan to steal it.

The data supports the hypothesis that d/Deaf students from NTID will not experience a higher rate of victimization from property crimes when compared to hearing students from RIT, and, therefore, the null hypothesis is accepted.

Victimization will reflect some degree of disability exploitation

Attempting to determine whether or not a person's unique physical characteristics play a role in his/her selection for victimization is a difficult undertaking. In an effort to capture the most reliable information, the researcher first queried respondents on the location of the criminal act, believing that such information could provide valuable insight into locales of greatest vulnerability. Secondly, given the possibility that during the commission of the act, *something* may have occurred that suggested to the victims that they were specifically selected because of their deafness, respondents were queried about

Table 5.17:
Locations and Frequency (in raw numbers)
Of sexually based offenses, for Deaf/HOH students

Sexual Crime	Home[1]	School[2]	Van/Car	In Bed	Outside	Friend's House	Other	No Info	Total
Movies	2		1				2		5
Touching	3[58]	2	1	2	2	4	2	2	18
Rubbing	3	2	1			2		2	10
Fellatio	1		1			2		2	6
Rape	1	2				1	1	1	6
Total	13	6	4	2	2	9	5	7	45

1   Home is inclusive of home and dorm where respondents identified "dorm room" in the "other" category

2   It is unclear whether or not the students checked off school to mean dorm room, so this category is treated separately, although it is possible that school means dorm room.

whether or not *they* believed that they were targeted because of their deafness. Together, these pieces of information (if provided) were used to determine whether or not target selective actions were employed on the part of the offender.

It is hard to argue that target selection was occurring if the victim doesn't even believe it to be true. In fact, the reported data seems to suggest that the Deaf/HOH students are not being specifically targeted.

---

[58]   Two respondents identified "in your bed" -- presumably located in one's home and one additional student identified "bathroom" as a location of assault which again, based on additional data provided (offender is identified as a sibling) is assumed to be the house bathroom.

Sexually-Based Offenses

In general, the sexually based offenses show evidence of target selection for the lesser intrusive crimes and more opportunity for the more serious offenses. For instance, while "home" and "friend's house" are consistently identified as areas where the d/Deaf students were most vulnerable to sexual touching without permission and sexual rubbing without permission, the crimes of fellatio and rape appeared to occur in more random locations, suggesting that those offenses were governed more by opportunity than by selective targeting.

Home, as the location of greatest vulnerability (29 % overall), is consistent with existing research (DAWN, 1998). The next area of greatest vulnerability as reported on this survey is a "friend's house" since 20 % of all of the sexual incidents took place at a friend's house. It is the researcher's observation that home and friend's house represent areas with a certain degree of intimacy, as opposed to the four other possible locations or those additionally identified (*i.e.,* nightclub, YMCA, work, etc.) for assault.

The level of intimacy required to gain access to one's home or to a friend's house implies that the offender is engaging in rationalized targeting behaviors since the offender is likely to know the victim and, therefore, be aware of the deafness. Therefore, the researcher believes that the reported data supports the research hypothesis with respect to sexual touching without permission.

As is the case with the sexual touching without permission, "home" is the area of greatest vulnerability in the case of sexual rubbing without permission, and a "friend's house" was also identified as the second most vulnerable location. Therefore, once again, the researcher believes that the research hypothesis is supported with respect to sexual rubbing without permission.

With respect to fellatio, the respondents report believing that they <u>are</u> being selected for victimization as a function of their deafness, which may be a result of the higher percentage of male victims. Aside from this gender possibility, it is unclear why the students' opinions have changed regarding the role of disability in the victimization. What is clear is that as the severity of the criminal act increases, the victim's willingness to part with specific details decreases.

Two of the five students have provided no information regarding their victimizations, other than to report that they occurred (both male victims). The remaining three students identify a variety of assault locations including "friend's house", "on way home" and "dorm". Again, the researcher believes that the research hypothesis is supported with respect to being forced to put one's mouth on the sexual organs of another, in large measure because the 40 % of the victims reported believing they were specifically targeted because of their deafness.

With respect to rape, a resistance on the part of the students to share specific details regarding the incident is again noticed. Two of the six students provided no information regarding their victimizations other than to report that they occurred (both male victims). The other four respondents identified four different locations "friend's house", "YMCA", "school" and "work" as the locations of assault. The seemingly random locations appear to suggest that these crimes were crimes of opportunity rather than selection. Therefore, in this instance, the researcher believes that deafness was a not a target selective factor, and further, that not enough data exists to support the research hypothesis with respect to forced penetration.

Violent, Intimate Offenses

The determination of whether or not one was selected to be robbed or assaulted as a function of his/her disability is a difficult undertaking. Similar to the analysis employed in the sexual crimes section, additional information was relied upon to determine whether or not the victim was *selected* on the basis of his/her disability, or because of some other factor.

With respect to robbery, there were eleven separate incidents reported by d/Deaf students. Seven of the events occurred only once, strangers were involved in five of the events, six of the victims did not list the location of the assaults, one victim identified "the tunnel[59]", and the three reported home/dorm as the location of the assault. Also, many of the items that were taken suggest impulse actions (*i.e.,* jewelry, cash, computer equipment, Playstation). In light of what was reported, the researcher believes it is impossible to determine target selection and, therefore, does not believe the research hypothesis is supported with respect to theft with injury (robbery).

With respect to the incidences of simple assault, eleven of the incidences occurred between victims and offenders who knew each other, and the information provided suggested that at least four of the incidences involved domestic violence. Further, several of the singular encounters occurred in bar/restaurants or outdoors by known people which suggests involvement of some alcohol (although that specific question was not asked on the survey). Perhaps most telling was that only two individuals claimed that they were targeted because of their disability: one of whom was involved in an abusive relationship with a boyfriend, and the other was assaulted by "friends" at school; yet, both victims chose not to identify the hearing status of their attackers.

Based on the reported data, the researcher does not believe that target selective behaviors were employed by the offenders and determines that the research hypothesis is not supported.

With respect to aggravated assault, six Deaf/HOH students reported seven separate incidents whereupon the victim was attacked with a weapon. Four students did not believe that they were specifically targeted as a function of their disability. In fact, one was accosted seemingly at random in "State Island"[60]; one respondent answered the question but provided no additional details; one respondent reported being attacked in a bar/restaurant by a stranger; and four incidents were described as taking place between two known persons having an argument (*i.e.,* boyfriend/girlfriend, neighbor, etc.).

---

[59] An underground network of pathways linking education buildings to one another
[60] Researcher believes that subject meant to write "Staten Island".

Given what was reported above, the data fails to support the research hypothesis with respect to target selective behaviors and aggravated assault.

Deaf students victimized by individuals they know more often than hearing students

Because the Deaf community is relatively small and insular, the researcher hypothesizes that the majority of victims will know their attackers.

A total of 51 sexual incidents were reported, eight from the hearing student population and 43 from the Deaf/HOH student population. Of those 51 incidents, students indicated familiarity with the offender in 37 % (19) of the cases. Twenty-four cases had no information provided, of which 79 % came from Deaf/HOH respondents. Reasons why respondents chose not to identify the specific relationship vary and may include embarrassment, fear of the offender, or fear that the offender may be harmed.

Sexual Offenses

Table 5.18 provides details regarding the information that was reported by both the hearing and the Deaf/HOH students regarding whether the offender was known to them. Statistical exploration shows no significant finding between the groups, which may be a reflection of the small sample sizes.

Table 5.18
Known Offenders, Sexual Offenses
For Hearing and Deaf/HOH students

Crimes	Hearing Students		Deaf/HOH Students		Missing	Total
	No	Yes	No	Yes		
Showing Movies				3	2	5
Sexual Touching	1	2	3	7	10	23
Sexual Rubbing			3	4	2	9
Fellatio				1	4	5
Rape			1	2	6	9
TOTAL	1	2	7	17	24	51

Hearing students reported a total of eight sexual incidents, yet only provided offender details for three (38%), of which offenders were known to the victim in two cases (*i.e.,* female babysitter and acquaintance-male). Conversely, the Deaf/HOH students reported a total of 43 sexual incidents, and 24 (56%) students provided details regarding the relationship with the offender. Of those 24, 17 (71%) of the victims knew their offender, some even providing detailed information such as "mom's boyfriend", "neighbor – male" or "brother".

With respect to the information provided from the Deaf/HOH students regarding the relationship with sexual offenders, 71% indicated that they knew their offender, as opposed to only 25% of the hearing students.

Violent, Person-to-Person Offenses

The nature and degree of physical contact necessary to perpetrate an intimate crime as legally defined, presupposes that the victim may have an opportunity to view their offender.

Table 5.19
Known Offenders, Violent Crime
For Hearing and Deaf/HOH students

Crimes	Hearing Students		Deaf/HOH Students		Missing	Total
	No	Yes	No	Yes		
Robbery			4	7	3	14
Simple Assault	1	1	4	10		16
Agg. Assault			4	1	3	8
TOTAL	1	1	12	18	6	38

Table 5.19 details the information provided for the three separate crimes inclusive of this section (theft with injury, simple assault, and aggravated assault) reveal a total of 38 separate incidents, three from the hearing student population and 35 from the Deaf/HOH student population. Of those 38 incidents, students indicated familiarity with the offender in 50 % (19) of the cases. Six cases had no information provided, of which five (83%) came from Deaf/HOH respondents. The result is that one (3%) hearing student and 18 (47%) Deaf/HOH students knew their offenders, and in some cases, specifically identified them, *i.e.,* Deaf fraternity members, boyfriend, father.

Additionally, data was also collected based on the respondents who identified that they did not know the offender. One (3%) hearing student responded that he/she did not know the offender, as did twelve (32%) of the Deaf/HOH students.

With respect to the information provided from the Deaf/HOH students regarding the relationship with violent offenders, 47% indicated that they knew their offender, as opposed to only 3% of the hearing students[61].

---

[61]   It should be noted that the hearing sample is very small and a larger sample may alter the findings.

Property Offenses

In general, property crime is not directed toward a specific person or persons, rather the goal is to obtain, typically through illegal means, an object or item of one's desire. In most cases, there is no physical or direct contact with another person so it is not anticipated that the victims will be able to identify the offender.

Table 5.20
Known offenders, Property Crime Victimization
For Hearing and Deaf/HOH students

Crimes	Hearing Students		Deaf/HOH Students		Missing	Total
	No	Yes	No	Yes		
Personal Theft	13	2	12	9	3	39
Burglary	6		10	6	2	24
Property Theft			3		7	10
Motor Vehicle Theft	2		1			3
Forgery	1		2	1	2	4
TOTAL	22	2	28	16	12	80

Table 5.20 details the information provided for the five separate crimes inclusive of this section (personal theft, burglary, property theft, motor vehicle theft, and forgery) and reveals a total of 80 separate incidents, 24 from the hearing student population and 44 from the Deaf/HOH student population. Of those 80 incidents, students indicated familiarity with the offender in only 23% (18) of the cases. Twelve cases had no information provided, of which two (17%) came from the hearing respondents and 10 (83%) from the Deaf/HOH respondents. The result is that only two (3%) hearing students and 16 (20%) Deaf/HOH students knew the offenders, and in some cases, chose to specifically identify them, *i.e.,* family friend, brother, uncle.

Additionally, data was also collected based on the respondents who identified that they did not know the offender. Twenty-two (28%)

hearing student responded that they did not know the offender, as did 28 (35%) of the Deaf/HOH students.

With respect to the information provided from the Deaf/HOH students regarding the relationship with property offenders, the majority of both populations indicated that they did not know the offenders. This finding is expected since most victims would not necessarily know the offenders since for the most part, thefts represent crimes of opportunity and often occur in the absence of the victim.

Deaf will report a higher rate of victimization from other Deaf

The proximity hypothesis supports the hypothesis that since Deaf/HOH persons often reside in geographic areas close to other Deaf/HOH persons for social reasons, they would report a high rate of victimization from other Deaf persons. This is also supported by contemporary theories (equivalent group hypothesis) that accept as true that "all persons have some probability of committing a crime and can be criminal one moment and non-criminal the next" (Clarke and Felson, 2004:10). This hypothesis is further supported by the recognized insular nature of the d/Deaf community.

Research in the d/Deaf community is consistently plagued by the general distrust that the d/Deaf have of hearing people (Chaugh, 1983; Kannapel, 1983), as well as a general reluctance to share information that might embarrass them or other d/Deaf people, or could bring shame upon the community (Lipton, Goldstein, Fahnbulleh & Gertz, 1996).

This research attempts to ameliorate any concerns regarding possible exploitation or harm that the respondents might fear would befall d/Deaf offenders, given that the data was provided to hearing researchers. Implementation of this sensitive line of questioning required that the hearing status of the offender be asked in the least threatening manner possible. To achieve that end, the question was inserted into the satisfaction portion of each crime on the survey. Unfortunately, this may introduce a challenge to reliability, because if the victim claimed that he/she did not report the criminal incident to anyone, then conceivably, he/she would not proceed to answer that portion of the question. While this was not always the case, the information regarding offender deafness was significantly less than what we had hoped for, evidenced by the fact that overall, 49 % of the questions regarding the hearing status of the offender was left blank.

Table 5.21
Offender Hearing Status, Sexual Offenses
Against Deaf/HOH students

Crimes	Occurrences Reported by Deaf Students		Offender Hearing Status		Missing
	Total Events	Knew offender	H	D	
Showing Movies	4	3	1	2	1
Sexual Touching	17	7	6	2	9
Sexual Rubbing	9	4	4	2	3
Fellatio	5	1	1		4
Rape	8	2	1	1	6
TOTAL	43	17	13	7	23

Table 5.21 suggests that of the identified offenders, 16% of the Deaf victims were sexually victimized by other Deaf, as compared to 30% of the Deaf victims victimized by hearing offenders. This appears to suggest that d/Deaf persons are more vulnerable to hearing offenders with respect to sexually based offenses – this finding does not support the research hypothesis. However, this data must be viewed with caution as 53 % of the information regarding the hearing status of the offender was not provided. Better response rates, better question placement in the survey, or larger sample sizes may change the finding.

Table 5.22
Offender Hearing Status, Violent Offenses
Against Deaf/HOH students

Crimes	Occurrences Reported by Deaf Students		Offender Hearing Status		Missing
	Total Events	Knew offender	H	D	
Robbery	14	7	6	3	5
Simple Assault	14	10	9	3	2
Agg. Assault	7	1	4		3
TOTAL	35	18	19	6	10

Table 5.22 suggests that of the identified offenders, 17% of the Deaf victims were violently assaulted by other Deaf, compared to 54% of the Deaf victims victimized by hearing offenders. This suggests that d/Deaf persons are more vulnerable to hearing offenders with respect to violent assaults and does not support the research hypothesis. This finding is not wholly unexpected since most personal, violent offenses occur in social settings, where the Deaf and hearing might congregate (*i.e.,* bar/restaurant, concert, etc.). Still, that 54% of assaults against Deaf are perpetrated by hearing may offer future research guidance.

Table 5.23
Offender Hearing Status, Property Crimes
Against Deaf/HOH Students

Crimes	Occurrences Reported by Deaf Students		Offender Hearing Status		Missing
	Total Events	Knew offender	H	D	
Personal Theft	24	9	13		11
Burglary	18	6	10		8
Property Theft	7		2		5
Vehicle Theft	1		1		
Forgery	3	1	2		2
TOTAL	53	16	28	0	26

Table 5.23 indicates that none of the property offenders identified by Deaf victims were Deaf, and 53 % of the hearing offenders were known to their victims. This appears once again to suggest that d/Deaf persons are more vulnerable to hearing offenders with respect to property crimes, a finding that does not support the research hypothesis.

The answers to these inquiries have critical applications to the development of policies and programs geared at reinforcing one's ability to maintain a safe existence and should definitely be addressed in any future research efforts.

NTID students will have a higher rate of repeat or chronic victimization compared to RIT students

Tables 5.24, 5.25 and 5.26 present data regarding the total number of victimizing incidents for Deaf and hearing students. There were a total of 133 victimizing incidents – inclusive of sexual, violent, and property crimes -- reported by Deaf students from NTID, and 35 total incidents reported by hearing students from RIT.

Further analysis explored whether Deaf or hearing students faced a greater vulnerability to repeat or chronic victimization for particular types of crime. Tables 5.24 and 5.25 illustrate that for each of the criminal categories, the percentage of students who were Deaf who reported multiple victimizations exceeded that of hearing students. However, d/Deaf students faced a particular vulnerability with respect to sexual and violent crimes. The findings are consistent with existing research that reports that individuals with disabilities are victimized more often and for longer periods of time (Young, et. al., 1997) than their non-disabled counterparts.

Table 5.24
Rates of Repeat or Chronic Victimization,
For Sexual Offenses, for Deaf/HOH and Hearing students

Crimes	Deaf Students		Hearing Students		Missing	Total
	Singular Events	Repeat Events	Singular Events	Repeat Events		
Movies	1	1			3	5
Touching	10	6	3	2	2	23
Rubbing	4	3			2	9
Fellatio	1	2			2	5
Rape	4	2	1		1	8
TOTAL	20	14	4	2	10	50

The data indicated that of the 34 sexually based incidents against Deaf students, 20 (59 %) occurred only one time and 14 (41 %) of Deaf students reported repeat or chronic victimization, as opposed to only 33 % of the hearing student population. These findings should be viewed with caution since 20% of the victims of sexual offenses did not provide information regarding the frequency of their victimization. However, the data that was reported does support the research hypothesis that d/Deaf students will experience increased vulnerability to chronic/repeat sexual victimization.

Table 5.25
Rates of Repeat or Chronic Victimization,
For Violent Offenses, for Deaf/HOH and Hearing students

Crimes	Deaf Students		Hearing Students		Missing	Total
	Singular Events	Repeat Events	Singular Events	Repeat Events		
Robbery	8	5			1	14
Simple Assault	7	8	2			17
Aggravated Assault	4	2			2	8
TOTAL	19	15	2	0	3	39

Table 5.25 shows that the reported data indicated that 34 violent crimes were perpetrated against students who were Deaf, of those crime, 19 (56 %) occurred only once and 14 (44 %) Deaf students reported repeat or chronic victimization, as opposed to none of the hearing student population. Only three cases (8 %) had missing data. Based upon the information provided, it appears that the research hypothesis that d/Deaf students will experience increased vulnerability to chronic/repeat violent assaults is supported.

Table 5.26
Rates of Repeat or Chronic Victimization,
For Property Crimes, for Deaf/HOH and Hearing students

Crimes	Deaf Students		Hearing Students		Missing	Total
	Singular Events	Repeat Events	Singular Events	Repeat Events		
Pers. Theft	14	7	10	5	3	39
Burglary	9	8	3	3		23
Prop. Theft	5	2	2	1		10
MVT	1		2			3
Forgery	3			1		4
TOTAL	32	17	17	10	3	79

Reported data indicates that there were 49 property crimes perpetrated against students who were Deaf, 32 (65 %) occurred only one time and 17 (35 %) of Deaf students reported repeat or chronic victimization, which is comparable to the 37% of the hearing student population who reported multiple property victimizations. Only three cases (4 %) had missing data. Based upon the information provided, it appears that the research hypothesis that d/Deaf students will experience increased vulnerability to repeat property crimes is not supported.

Measures of Social Disenfranchisement

A key foundation of this study is the belief that by virtue of their difference, Deaf/HOH are denied power positions in society (either through cultural or medical exclusion – see Chapter Two herein). The researchers sought to evaluate the depth of Deaf/HOH involvement with mainstream culture by devising a basic quiz (see Part II, Appendix

C) that would measure the level of knowledge Deaf/HOH have with the criminal justice system.

This quiz is based on a belief that a good deal of knowledge regarding society and its agents is acquired through pop-culture media outlets such as television shows, print ads or press programs. Since pop cultural outlets, by definition, appeal mainly to members of the mainstream culture, sub-cultural members should not acquire the same level of information. The importance of this measure is in recognition of the long term implications of alienation from the criminal justice system and its operations, which include, but are not limited to, failure to report a criminal event, distrust of first responders, fear of the legal system, and an ignorance of the financial recovery programs or treatment options that may exist for victims of crime.

Figure 5.1 illustrates the overall performance for the Deaf/HOH and Hearing students. As can be seen, the none of the students who were Deaf scored above 87 % (13/15), while the mean average score for those students was 57 (sd = 2.50). Conversely, the none of the hearing students scored *below* 40% (6/15), except for the three hearing students who did not take the quiz at all, and the mean average score for those students was 74 (sd = 2.91). This finding suggests that hearing students possess more knowledge about the basic services and functions of the criminal justice system than do their Deaf/HOH counterparts.

Additionally, this study is able to make a significant contribution towards resolving this inequity by analyzing the scores for each question. Careful review of individual question scores allow the criminal justice field to identify what parts of the system are least understood, and facilitate the development of programs specifically catered to those information gaps.

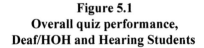

Figure 5.1
Overall quiz performance,
Deaf/HOH and Hearing Students

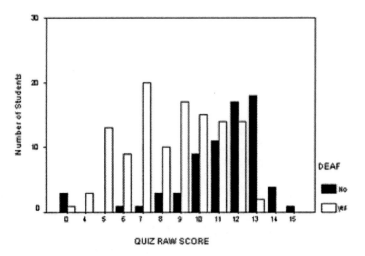

Table 5.27 compares the performance of d/Deaf and Hearing students for each question on the quiz. From Table 5.27, one can easily determine the areas where the transmission of information does not penetrate marginal populations. For example, although 91 % of Deaf/HOH students answered correctly that if a victim, one has the right to assistance during the trial; one must be careful to consider that while he/she answered correctly, this may be misleading. It is possible that the Deaf/HOH answered on the basis of their special circumstance (needing an interpreter) rather than demonstrating knowledge that victims are entitled to services from a victim advocate.

Table 5.27
Chi Square Tests of Significance for
Individual Quiz Questions, for Deaf/HOH and Hearing Students

Quiz Question	Directional tendency of correct questions N= 189	df	X² value	p value
If victim, hire attorney	**D(48%) > H (9%)**	1	**30.598****	.000
Judge decide b/4 trial	**D(43%) < (86%)**	1	**33.470****	.000
Define exclusionary rule	**D(37%) < H(80%)**	1	**32.931****	.000
Titles - District Attorney	**D (52%) < H(77%)**	1	**11.675****	.001
Define "law"	*D (65%) > H (48%)*	*1*	*5.516**	*.019*
Arrest = guilt	**D (69%) < H(96%)**	1	**18.698****	.000
Victim assistance	*D (91%) > H (77%)*	*1*	*6.320**	*.012*
Assist for robbery victim	**D (48%) < H(82%)**	1	**20.738****	.000
Plea bargaining	D (20%) < H (28%)	1	1.522	.217
Prosecutor job descrip.	**D (52%) < H(89%)**	1	**26.949****	.000
Define "felony"	*D (80%) < H (91%)*	*1*	*4.160**	*.041*
Define "penitentiary"	*D (81%) < H (93%)*	*1*	*4.873**	*.027*
Define "acquitted"	**D (32%) < H(87%)**	1	**54.055****	.000
Conviction	**D (39%) < H(68%)**	1	**14.527****	.000
Crime reporting	D (89%) < H (93%)	1	.530	.467

D = d/Deaf students; H = Hearing students

* = significant at the 0.05 level; ** = significant at the 0.01 level

The Deaf/HOH demonstrated knowledge about whom to call to report a crime as 89% correctly identified 911. It should be noted, however, that some of the students who answered the question incorrectly, did so because they listed a "relay operator" as their answer. Specifically in the Deaf community, this may not be incorrect if they suspect that the 911 Operators may not be able to respond to their call. As a matter of fact, a Department of Justice website admits that "Often an agency has purchased a sufficient number of telecommunication devices (TDD), but lacks personnel trained in how to use them" (www.usdoj.gov/crt/ada/pubs/911.txt).

Deaf/HOH students also demonstrate a familiarity with specific vocabulary within the criminal justice system; for instance, "felony" and "penitentiary" were understood at 80 % and 81 %, respectively. In fact, the only vocabulary word that presented a challenge to the students who are Deaf was "acquittal" as only 32 % of those students got it correct. This may be a result of the fact that "acquittal" does not translate into sign language, rather "got off" or "let go" would be used.

Specific areas that proved challenging to Deaf/HOH students include (1) general procedures employed in the resolution of a case, such as plea bargaining (20 % correct), or conviction (39 % correct), (2) the specific roles and responsibilities of the criminal justice system personnel (52 % correct), and (3) the professional responsibilities of courtroom personnel, specifically the prosecutor (48 % correct), and the judge (43 % correct).

Plea Bargaining

While only 20 % of students who were Deaf answered this question correctly, to be fair, only 28 % of the hearing students answered it correctly, which suggests that the general principles of plea bargaining are elusive for both Deaf and hearing populations. This is also supported by the fact that the observed difference between the groups did not amount to a statistically significant finding. However, familiarity with plea bargaining is crucial to establishing a degree of confidence and trust in the criminal justice system. Plea bargaining (or plea negotiation) is used in over 90% of the charges filed (Anderson & Newman, 1998:242), and generally involves the defendant pleading guilty, most often to a less serious crime than the one originally charged.

Failure to understand the role and function of plea bargaining in our system can lead victims to believe that the Judge has let someone "get off", that the prosecutor didn't do his/her job or worse, that the police didn't believe the complainant. Such misunderstandings are a reality. In fact, recognition of the need for victim advocates is firmly based in the recognition that victims did not understand what was happening in court, and that they required assistance to understand the adjudicative procedures.

Identification of this information gap reinforces the hypothesis being tested and clearly demonstrates an area of needed intervention. If professionals running the criminal justice system are genuinely attempting to extend equal access of the justice system to the Deaf/HOH community, they must direct significant educational efforts toward reducing the gaps in information that separate the cultures.

Police responsibilities and functions

Since 31 % of students who are Deaf believed that an arrest was equivalent to guilt, as compared to only 4 % the hearing students, the researcher sees this as an area of necessary intervention. It is directly connected to the level of trust that the Deaf/HOH has with the police and may have a direct effect whether or not they choose to report a crime.

Also, 63 % of the Deaf/HOH students were unaware that there are sanctions for law enforcement if they do not do their job properly. The exclusionary rule, per se, was not something that would be known, but it was anticipated that most would be aware that if the police did not do their job properly, collected evidence could be excluded. As a matter of fact, only 20 % of the hearing students had this question wrong, suggesting that most hearing students did know that the police could be sanctioned.

Prosecutor responsibilities and Functions

Just over half (52 %) of the students who are Deaf believe that the victim is responsible for hiring his/her own attorney, as opposed to only nine percent of the hearing students. Additionally, 48 % of the Deaf/HOH students were unable to correctly describe a prosecutor's job function, supported also by the finding that only 39 % were able to identify who won the case if an offender was found guilty.

These findings suggest that the role of the prosecutor, both as guardian of state law and advocate for the victim(s), must become a key focus of any outreach program directed at the Deaf community.

Judicial responsibilities and functions

Fifty-seven percent of the students who are Deaf believe that a judge determines before the start of a trial who s/he thinks is being truthful, as opposed to only 12 % of the hearing students. This highlights the fact that the Deaf/HOH are unfamiliar with the impartial role of the judge, and that can lead to heightened mistrust of the courtroom proceedings. This mistrust often manifests itself in the Deaf/HOH choosing not to involve the legal system and, as a result, increases their isolation and may render some victims helpless to protect themselves.

In summary, there was no observed difference between the two groups for plea bargaining and reporting a crime, suggesting that both the Deaf and hearing students have a firm understanding of who to call for assistance following a crime and a relatively   equal degree of misunderstanding with respect to plea bargaining.

The data also showed that the Deaf students outperformed hearing students on the questions addressing whether or not victims have to hire their own attorneys; victim rights to assistance and the definition of a "law". Also, the observed differences were statistically significant (α = 0.05 level, df = 1).

For the remaining ten questions (67 % of the quiz) which addressed a variety of issues within the criminal justice system, such as basic definitions, procedures and roles and responsibilities of person, the hearing students outperformed the Deaf students. The observed differences were statistically significant for the most part at the α = .001 level (df = 1).

Such findings support the research hypothesis that the Deaf will demonstrate significant disenfranchisement from the criminal justice system. Table 5.18 also shows the findings to be mostly statistically significant (with the exception of plea bargaining and crime reporting), so the researcher rejects the null hypothesis in favor of the alternative.

Deaf will be dissatisfied with services from the criminal justice system

This study attempts to employ a modified satisfaction survey in an effort to determine whether or not persons who are Deaf are satisfied with the level of services received from the criminal justice system. Each criminal incident (13) included a series of eight questions[62]:

1. If you told someone, was your complaint ever investigated by police?
2. If the police investigated, was someone arrested?
3. If someone was arrested, were you interviewed by the state's lawyer?
4. If someone was arrested, did he/she admit guilt and get punishment?
5. If someone was arrested, did he/she go to court?
6. If case did go to trial, was the person found guilty?
7. If person found guilty, did he/she go to jail?

The first consideration in designing this section was to provide indicators to provide the researcher the opportunity to test the veracity of statements made up to that point. For instance, if a victim claimed earlier that they did not report or tell anyone about the criminal incident, then it is highly suspect if the crime was investigated or prosecuted. This cross-checking method allowed the researcher to determine reliability of responses in some cases, and in others to better gauge the level of comprehension regarding system operations.

What became apparent shortly after the administration of this survey was that the questions posed above assumed a factor that was unlikely

---

[62] One question does not fit the criteria of a satisfaction item, so it is not included in this discussion.

in felony cases -- namely that the crime would have had to occur, be investigated and adjudicated within the prior thirteen months in order for the victim to be able to answer the questions posed above. "The wheels of justice grind slowly" is not simply a phrase but often a reality, and it is highly unlikely that a felony crime could have been adjudicated in the short time frame of just one year. It is primarily for this reason that it was clear that the research hypothesis could not be tested on the basis of actual responses, and therefore, the reported data is deemed inconclusive.

Still, while there are examples where answers to specific questions may not be supportive of the individual research question at hand, the inference – while perhaps not statistically sound – is indeed reflective of the general problem. For instance, with respect to the specific research question of satisfaction with the criminal justice system services following a victimizing incident, it is clear that the actual responses suffer from challenges on many levels, including but not limited to:

- Comprehensive understanding – Chapter Five details the responses which clearly indicate a general misunderstanding or lack of knowledge regarding how the criminal justice system functions in terms of individual roles, responsibilities, and obligations to both the victim and the offender; and

- Sequential realities – as mentioned above, it is virtually impossible – save for a plea bargain or a guilty plea for a felony case to occur, be investigated, prosecuted, and adjudicated in the short time frame of less than one year.

However, a more subtle measure of police satisfaction could be inferred by the number of times the police are called by a Deaf or hearing victim following a criminal incident. Table 5.28[63] presents a reflection of how often respondents listed the "police" as the person they chose to call upon for assistance. The students who are Deaf told 179 people about the crimes that happened to them, while the hearing students told 75 people about the crimes that happened to them. The Deaf students only notified the police in 28 circumstances, representing 16 % of the time. The hearing students didn't report to the police much more than that; they notified the police in 16 circumstances, representing 21 % of the time – only 5 % more often than the Deaf.

It could be argued, however, that both the Deaf and hearing students do not rely upon the police for assistance immediately following a criminal event. However, whether or not that lack of reliance is a function of satisfaction is unclear, which is why the hypothesis finding must remain inconclusive.

---

[63]   The table is presented in a modal format since respondents were able to select more than one person when indicating whom they turned to for assistance, and because of the dichotic nature of the question, it is impossible to determine how often, how many or the priority of whom they selected for assistance.

Table 5.28
Modal analysis of victim notification following victimization,
By crime classification

	Didn't tell anyone	Family	Friends	Staff	Police/ campus sec.	Priest / Rabbi	Other	Don't want to tell	Blank
Since January 2002, did someone force you to watch movies, pictures or videos showing the sex act (with adults, children or both in the movie) when you didn't want to?									
Deaf	1	3	3						
Hearing	1								
Since January 2002, did someone touch your sexual organs (penis, vagina or breasts) without asking you?									
Deaf	2	6	8		2	1	1	2	
Hearing	4	2	1	1	1				
Since January 2002, did someone rub or massage your sexual areas (penis, vagina or breasts) without asking you?									
Deaf	2	4	4	1	1				
Hearing									
Since January 2002, did someone force you to put your mouth on their sexual organs (penis, vagina or breasts) without asking you?									
Deaf		1	2	2					2
Hearing									
Since January 2002, did someone put something in your vagina or rectum (penis or object) without asking you?									
Deaf	1		2					2	2
Hearing		1	1	1	1				
Since January 2002, did someone steal something that belonged to you and hurt you to get it?									
Deaf	3	1	2		3			1	1
Hearing									
Since January 2002, did someone attack you (i.e., punch or kick) and hurt you (i.e., cuts, bruises, broken bones)?									
Deaf	1	7	6	1	2				4

	Didn't tell anyone	Family	Friends	Staff	Police/campus sec.	Priest / Rabbi	Other	Don't want to tell	Blank
Hearing		1	2						
Since January 2002, did someone attack you with a weapon (i.e., baseball bat, rock, gun, knife, etc)?									
Deaf		4	4	1	2		1	1	
Hearing									1
Since January 2002, did someone steal something from you without hurting you, (i.e., purse, backpack, laptop)?									
Deaf	2	15	14	4	5		2		
Hearing	1	8	11	3	8	1	2		
Since January 2002, did someone steal something from inside your home when you weren't home, (i.e., jewelry, TV, computer, stereo, etc)?									
Deaf		8	9	2	8		1		
Hearing		5	4		3		1		
Since January 2002, did someone steal something from outside your home without your knowing, (i.e., bike)?									
Deaf		6	4		2				1
Hearing		1	2		1				
Since January 2002, did someone steal your car or motorcycle?									
Deaf					1				
Hearing		1	1	1	1				1
Since January 2002, did someone sign your check and steal your money?									
Deaf		3	3	2	1		1		
Hearing		1	1		1				
DEAF TOTAL	12	58	61	13	28	1	6	6	10
HEARING TOTAL	6	20	23	6	16	1	3	0	2

Still, in spite of the statistical challenges to this question, Table 5.28 clearly shows that family and friends are the primary source of support for Deaf respondents following victimization (32 % and 34 % respectively), indicating that any program that may be developed to assist a d/Deaf crime victim should actively seek inclusion of friends and family. This does *not* mean that the friends and family should be used as interpreters or communicators for the d/Deaf victim. Factors such as secondary victimization and related trauma confound the ability of the friend or family member to interpret effectively. They should be treated as corollary victims and not be forced to assume the role of communicator.

The criminal justice system will fail to adequately respond to post-victimization needs of persons who Deaf

This research hypothesis cannot be addressed by the data, and therefore, is deemed inconclusive. The combination of factors, namely that the police are frequently not notified by the victim of criminal acts, and that when notified, the time frame restrictions suggest that the case would not have reached resolution at the time of this survey administration. As a result, the research hypothesis could not be tested, and therefore, is deemed inconclusive.

CHAPTER SIX
Research Contributions

Discussion of Broader Findings

The analyses presented in Chapter Five offer considerable direction and insight for future research. The foundation of the specific findings and final conclusions herein is that any research that is to be undertaken within communities of persons with disabilities must reflect recognition of that community's unique cultural and social experience.

When ASL users represent the target population, the most critical element is the implementation of a linguistically sensitive document, because without that, any conclusions drawn from the data are suspect. Failure to recognize the unique language, syntax and vocabulary of Deaf language (ASL) and further, to adapt research instruments to meet those linguistic elements, will result in findings with little to no application to the target population.

This project used a blended written language (part ASL/part English), interpreting through ASL and Signed Pidgin English (SPE), and oralism to communicate the goals of the project, thereby recognizing and respecting that the d/Deaf population involves a culturally diverse group of people with different communication styles. The simultaneous implementation of a variety of communication methods ensure accurate and reliable data which can then be relied upon to provide critical information pertaining to crimes committed against the Deaf community.

Another specific result of this project is that while most contemporary efforts to study the victimization of vulnerable populations use the phrase "crimes against the disabled"; such a generic label denies the uniqueness of the person and the individual characteristics of the disability. Little mention is made in the literature suggesting that any effort to study vulnerable populations must have its own survey instrument. It is erroneous and misinformed to assume that a single survey instrument could successfully gather usable information from the Deaf, Blind, MR/DD, or any other sub-culture. *Each population must be addressed separately* to ensure valid and credible data.

Overall, this project illuminated that each sub-cultural community in American society employs some practice, behavior or attitude that protects it from being assumed completely into the main culture. It is, in effect, what sets them apart – it is *their* identity. Nonetheless, research tends to approach each group under investigation in the same manner thereby ensuring that findings are consistent. Strict adherence to scientific methodology however, may serve as a barrier to collecting the best possible data and to producing information truly useful to the population under study. Cultural sensitivity, therefore, should be valued as much as scientific integrity.

And finally, inclusive in the acceptance of target specific research efforts is the recognition that adapting research practices to fit particular situations is critical to ensure that the findings will be useful to the scientific community as well as the target community. Emerging methodologies, such as the one employed herein – Participant Active Research (PAR) – affords researchers the opportunity to engage in a "dialogue" that allows the "knowledge of the people [being studied] to produce a more profound understanding of the situation" (Reason, 1994:328). Such a dialogue almost guarantees that the findings will be recognized and useful to the population under study. What follows below are some specific recommendations for improving the handling and subsequent response to members of the Deaf community should they find themselves suddenly involved in the criminal justice system.

Public Policy Recommendations for the Criminal Justice System

The recommendations for the criminal justice system discussed below are derived generally from a consideration of how improving incident responses from law enforcement can benefit the target population following a crime and from an examination into the potential benefits of extending crime prevention programs to the target community.

The criminal justice system, at each level, must actively work to gain the trust of the d/Deaf community

Although the hypotheses explored herein regarding the effectiveness of law enforcement, and victim satisfaction with criminal justice system services were inconclusive, the responses implied that law enforcement and the criminal justice system are not viewed by d/Deaf victims as allies. A strained relationship between the d/Deaf population and law enforcement has existed for quite some time, and it follows that if the d/Deaf do not report crimes to begin with, then the other agencies in the criminal justice system cannot become activated. Some very real obstacles introduced by first responders (typically law enforcement) include:

- Assumptions of mental inferiority due to deafness;
- The tacit reluctance to hire interpreters[64];
- A lack of accessible and appropriately promoted information on services that exist for assaulted women; or
- The tendency to view women with a communications difficulty as not credible (Anello, 1998).

Such systemic practices are only compounded by the less obvious obstacles imposed by the d/Deaf community itself, such as:

---

[64] "Deaf Woman Files Suit Against New Braunfels", an article by staff writer Roger Croteau in The San Antonio Express-News, August 25, 2006

- A lack of knowledge regarding what behaviors constitute criminal acts;
- Fear of isolation from their community if the abuser is also Deaf (Anello, 1998); and
- A lack of understanding regarding the specific job responsibilities and professional or legal limitations of law enforcement.

Additionally, it cannot be ignored that the same pressures that create a barrier between law enforcement and Deaf victims also work to the advantage of many Deaf offenders. For example, Deaf individuals often are not arrested or issued citations, because communication barriers lead law enforcement authorities to ignore or overlook legal infringements (Guthmann, 2000). This misguided benevolence on the part of law enforcement serves only to perpetuate the 'lesser' status of the Deaf community within the general social framework. "Failing to provide basic accommodations to citizens who are deaf alienates them from their government, causes them to distrust those who are supposed to protect them, and makes them feel like second-class citizens," said Lucy Wood, regional managing attorney for Advocacy Inc., a nonprofit law firm that helps the disabled (Croteau, 2006).

Be aware of and sensitive to specific communication abilities and comprehension levels of the target audience

The current assumption that "writing it down," "speaking slowly," or "signing it" is simplistic to the point of ignorance and threatens to preserve the societal structure that actively works to alienate the d/Deaf community from the services needed for recovery following victimization. Employing specifically designed survey instruments promises that the information gathered from the d/Deaf population can then be used to revise procedures or protocols originally developed for hearing victims. Such revisions should take into account the cultural aspects of this silent population and when merged with empirical data, could result in more effective programs or practices that promise to improve the delivery of victim recovery services.[65]

Actively work to inform the Deaf community of research that tends to hold true over time and cross-culturally (i.e., victimization by known individuals and proneness to repeat victimization).

Within the d/Deaf student population surveyed, 60 % of respondents reporting some degree of sexual victimization, 47 % of respondents reporting some type of violent victimization and 44 % of respondents reporting some type of property crime were able to identify their offender.

The phenomenon of the victim knowing their offender is not unique to the Deaf population since contemporary victimization research has found that to be the case for all populations under study. What is important is that this risk factor must be conveyed to the community to alert them to the vulnerability that *everyone* faces from those known to them. Doing so may reduce anxiety and improve relations between law enforcement and persons who are Deaf during the initial phases of an investigation.

Such information is especially critical since law enforcement often consider persons known to the victim as potential offenders. If a person who is Deaf is not aware that most victims are assaulted by individuals known to them, they might not understand why the police are focusing on their friends or colleagues. That misunderstanding can easily lead to mistrust of the investigative procedures and subsequently either prevent a victim from reporting the crime or cause a victim to subconsciously impede an investigation under a misguided loyalty to their community.

---

[65] For example, an older Deaf adult may refuse attempts to gather or collect evidence if the interpreter seems too young, or is of another gender. Such refusal is often viewed by law enforcement as obstruction and may create uncomfortable and tense exchanges that further prevent successful intervention efforts.

The conclusions drawn from analysis of the findings, if addressed by the criminal justice system at large, virtually guarantees more effective methods of interviewing and obtaining evidence from any vulnerable population. It further ensures that Deaf victims will be more effective when testifying in court mainly because they will better understand how the process functions.

Public Policy Recommendations for Victim Service Agencies

The recommendations for victim service agencies discussed below are derived generally from a consideration of both the long-term and short-term benefits of immediate victim recovery efforts, as well as recognition of the active role that victim services can play in the implementation of programs designed to prevent victimization.

Educating persons who are Deaf as to the common risk factors for victimization (i.e., alcohol, late night activities, solitary outings, etc.) is critical for self-protection.

The rate of violent victimization within the d/Deaf student sample was high; d/Deaf students reported sexual victimization at twice that of hearing students, and while hearing students reported no victimization from robbery and aggravated assault, d/Deaf students reported 10 % and 5% (respectively); finally, Deaf/HOH students were targeted for simple assault at almost five times the rate of hearing students. These rates suggest that a lingually appropriate crime prevention program could significantly reduce the rate of violent victimization within the d/Deaf community. In fact, efforts currently underway to prevent sexual victimization within the Deaf community are showing preliminary evidence of success (Williams & White, 2001).

Additional benefits from such a program may include a reduced rate of victimization (see below) as some researchers have suggested that an initial victimization from violent crime is a warning signal for future violent victimization (Shaffer & Ruback, 2002). Therefore, successfully identifying risk factors and providing immediate post-victimization recovery assistance can significantly improve the health and safety of the target population.

Work aggressively towards administering victim recovery intervention efforts immediately following a victimizing incident.

Overall, forty-four percent of d/Deaf students reported repeat or chronic victimization, as opposed to only 35 % of hearing students, with sexual offenses and violent victimization showing the greatest rates of vulnerability. Current research has suggested that repeat victims might be especially suitable for interventions to prevent future victimization since prevailing research has shown that one incident of violent victimization may be a warning sign for future violent victimizations. The reasons behind this phenomenon range from psychologically based explanations, wherein the victim repeatedly places him/herself in environments similar to the initial one in an attempt to regain control (Freud, 1896; van der Kolk, 1989); to socially based explanations in that the environments frequented by the victim are conducive to violent crimes (Hindelang, et.al., 1978); and individually based theories, wherein the victim may be viewed as particularly vulnerable to victimization due to some identifying personal characteristic (von Hentig, 1948; Fattah, 1991).

Since crime victims are likely to experience depression, anxiety and physical health problems (Kilpatrick, et.al., 1985), it is important, on many levels, to improve recovery services offered to the population of crime victims. Najavits et. al. (1998) wrote that "Without trauma-informed intervention, there can exist a circular self-perpetuating cycle involving PTSD and substance abuse, where trauma leads to the development of PTSD symptoms, triggering the use of alcohol and drugs to cope..., resulting in higher likelihood of subsequent traumatic events and re-traumatization,... triggering heightened substance use and so on."

The policy implications of providing immediate assistance are many and cross several disciplines. It would appear that development and implementation of culturally sensitive intervention programs promises to prevent the further decline of the individual, as well as perhaps prevent future victimization.

Extend intervention programs to include friends and family.

Inclusion of friends and family is crucial to ensuring the effectiveness of any outreach effort since the data demonstrated that persons who are Deaf often contact friends and family immediately following a criminal event rather than law enforcement. Chapter Five includes a discussion regarding the lack of trust and confidence that the Deaf community has towards the police. Table 5.28 presents a modal analysis demonstrating who the d/Deaf victim is more likely to notify about what happened to them, of the 194 people that respondents identified as having told of their assault, 119 (61%) were friends and family. This suggests that any outreach program aimed at aiding this population must include the participation and education of friends and family, and the definition of such must be extended to include not only immediate family, but also friends, neighbors, caregivers, advocates, etc. (Rivers-Moore, 1992).

The findings herein stand to benefit not only the Deaf population, but to offer guidance to the criminal justice system as a whole, as well as provide valuable insight to the research community at large. Further, if the recommendations are acknowledged and implemented, future studies promise to provide data previously unavailable.

Study Limitations

Limitations for any study can be viewed as general and specific. General refers to limitations that are consistent with particular research methodologies; and specific are unique to the instant study. What follows is a brief discussion of the recognized limitations, both general and specific.

General limitations

In December 2000, NIJ published a report examining the issues of sexual victimization among college women (Fisher, et. al., 2000).

Researchers identified six limitations consistent with the research subject matter. Although this study diligently worked to overcome the obstacles described in this report, the researcher was unable to correct "the failure to use a randomly selected, national sample" and "to collect detailed information on what occurred during the victimizing incident" (Fisher, 2000:2).

The first limitation -- the collection of a randomly selected national sample -- is one that given this particular population, proves to be quite elusive. The limited access to and overall representation of d/Deaf[66] persons in college environments make this a challenging obstacle to overcome.

Further, the general impossibility of making direct observations of every individual in a population dictates that researchers must often collect data from a 'sample', and then use those observations to make inferences about the entire population. In order to draw conclusions from the sample that might apply to the entire population, it is best if the sample corresponds to the larger population on the characteristic(s) of interest, in this case, deafness.

The sampling method employed herein, convenience sampling, dictates that the representativeness of the general population of Deaf people cannot be known, and therefore, any findings pertain only to the sample population. As a result of this limitation, any implications drawn from this study are best considered in the context of university campuses and restricted to the variables examined herein. When applying the findings to other settings, careful consideration of the said restrictions (i.e., 18-24 year olds) should be employed to determine how applicable the findings may be for the intended purpose.

The second limitation – collecting detailed incident-specific information -- is one that was identified and recognized in this study,

---

[66] The term "d/Deaf" is used as representative of the sample population and is inclusive of culturally Deaf students and those students who prefer to employ hearing assistive devices.

and serious attempts were undertaken to correct that shortcoming. However, time constraints and language barriers prevented adequate addressing of these issues in this study, but future studies can definitely improve upon these shortcomings – especially studies that employ proven tactics from this project, i.e., using a CODA interpreter, providing an introductory sheet (in ASL), and altering survey questions in recommended ways.

With any self-report survey study, the most common limitation is with respect to recall error. The recognized and accepted challenges include: (1) memory – the respondent may simply not remember certain events which is especially true if the respondent has had multiple victimizations; (2) telescoping – where the respondent may not accurately recall when the incident actually occurred; and (3) exaggeration – where the respondent may have difficulty remembering each incident clearly, and, therefore, may inaccurately report the events. This can be especially true in situations of repeat or chronic victimization.

Other limitations to self-report studies include whether or not one chooses to participate, which could result in a sampling bias (Adler et. al., 1998:29). This study attempted to mitigate those problems by enlisting the support of the teachers and demonstrating flexibility to the circumstances, thereby enhancing the support of the students.

Specific Limitations

In terms of specific limitations, the researcher found that they manifested themselves in three main arenas: survey instrument, interview format, and use of official data reports, such as the National Crime Victimization Survey (NCVS).

Survey Instrument

As mentioned in Chapter Four, the survey instrument was developed and modelled from three existing surveys: the NCVS, the CAST-MR and a previous survey examining sexual abuse of d/Deaf adults (see Duvall, 1998). This survey instrument employed a close-ended, fixed alternative question format that provided a finite set of answers from which the respondent selected an answer. Closed-ended questions allow for easy standardization and use in statistical analysis (Fink, 1995). However, they can be challenging, in as much as the researcher must design choices that include all possible responses. As that reality is often impossible, use of such a format can arguably represent a limitation to the overall study.

This study attempts to compensate for this occurrence by providing an area for the respondent to provide additional information through an open-ended option – "other". Additionally, through the interpreter, the respondents were encouraged to write anywhere on the paper any information they felt was needed for clarity. The researcher believed that providing permission for writing anywhere on the survey would encourage the respondents to provide information spontaneously. It should be noted, however, that if future research is going to attempt a more open-ended format, then the overall length of the survey must be significantly shorter.

Chapter Four also discusses how researchers choosing to use Participant Action Research (PAR) must be willing to "design new instruments and techniques to gather data" (pg. 85). Therefore, the researcher chooses to include a brief discussion of the individual elements that were identified as improving the survey instrument were they to be changed:

- *Evaluate the need for the screening / headline question* – since the use of this question produced conflicting results, it was determined that the presentation (bold, large print) was viewed by respondents as a potential risk to confidentiality. In future efforts, the researcher recommends elimination of the headline question.

- *Be sure to use audience specific vocabulary / syntax* – although previously mentioned, it bears repeating. Careful consideration must be paid to the selection of questions (ensuring that they do not require a better than average understanding) and to the vocabulary used (ensuring that the vernacular is contemporary, maybe even employing a popular slang term, i.e., "slammer" or "joint" for prison/jail).

- *Be specific about what information the research is seeking.* For example, this survey queried respondents to identify "who" they chose to call following victimization. Upon review of the submitted data, it was determined that richer information would have been achieved if the respondent was asked to rate *sequentially* who they would have told first, second, third, etc.

- *Better operationalization of terms* (by the researcher) is needed – for example, it is unclear from the responses herein that the respondents understood the intended difference between identifying a "stranger" as the offender and selecting "don't know". Future efforts would need to determine whether or not the difference between those two options is necessary and if it is, clarify specifically under which circumstances each of the options should be used.

- *Limit the length and focus of the overall survey* – the survey herein was 53 pages. A shorter survey (no more than 10 pages recommended) would provide a richer data mine and ultimately result in the development of better policies and programs. Implementation of open-ended questions is encouraged to allow the respondent to provide more detail specific to their experiences.

Interview format

This study employed some unique methods designed to improve upon the above referenced limitations of the survey format. For instance, in an effort to address the concern of recall error, this survey used a specific temporal marker for each question – "Since January 1, 2002...." In translation, the interpreter referenced "New Year's Day last year" to confirm and reiterate the time frame. General findings were that since New Year's Day is memorable, the respondents were better able to recall incidents that happened within the past year.

Another interesting challenge to this study manifested itself on the first day of survey administration. It was noted that five respondents had not participated, and that several others gave very limited responses. The research team discussed what may be missing that would prevent the respondents from becoming "engaged" in the study. It was ultimately decided that the team had to help the respondents *see* the importance of the study, which would hopefully lead to increased participation. At that point, the researcher gathered several headlines from national papers regarding crimes against the d/Deaf community, the interpreter worked to provide a worksheet that could be understood by ASL signers (English words in ASL syntax) and had 200 copies made. Beginning day two, each student was handed a sheet upon entry into the classroom and left to read and discuss it for ten minutes before being introduced to the project. Every student actively participated from that point forward.

A limitation specific to this study was the reliance upon a third-party for communication. The inability to directly speak to individual respondents introduced the possibility that the interpreter may misunderstand the goal of the question, and as a result, mislead the respondents while communicating instructions or providing clarification. This study attempted to compensate for that limitation by having the interpreter not only actively participate in the construction of the survey instrument, but the researcher and interpreter arrived on-site one day prior to survey administration and went through the survey question-by-question to ensure that the interpreter fully understood the origin of each question and could answer any inquiry without bias.

The inability, because of confidentiality practices and to the large percentage of respondents who were unwilling to identify their victimizers, to corroborate any of the reported information introduced a possible limitation to validity. This study attempted to correct that limitation by providing a wide range of possible answers and encouraging respondents to write anywhere on the survey when a thought occurred to them. While some of respondents did make notes in margins, next to questions, or on the back of the sheets, future research should encourage a more open-ended format structure.

Official Data Reports

As mentioned above, this study also employed a secondary source of data for comparative purposes – the National Crime Victimization Survey (NCVS). As such, it is necessary to mention briefly the recognized and accepted limitations of the NCVS. First, given the nature of the self-report, survey format, it exhibits the same recall limitations as the instant study -- telescoping and recall. Additionally, because of the in-person nature of the survey (either face-to-face or over the phone), having a respondent fabricate an incident (to please the researcher) is a possibility.

And finally, it cannot be assumed that the data on the NCVS do not include persons who are d/Deaf because, while it may be highly unlikely, it is possible that they may be included in the household figures if someone else was reporting the crimes.

Future Research

This study suggests several areas for future research:

Compare the rates of victimization between the adults who are Deaf and the younger, residential school population.

The few studies that do explore victimization within the d/Deaf community focus on the institutionalized or residential school population. For example, in 2001, the *Seattle Post-Intelligencer* released a series of articles exposing an epidemic of sexual abuse taking place in residential schools for the Deaf. The articles focused national attention on the threats to d/Deaf children, but did little to identify what threats exist for d/Deaf adults.

These reports had little impact on the immediate study, given the age limitations of the instant study. Since the vulnerabilities facing d/Deaf youths in residential settings and adult d/Deaf students on a college campus are not necessarily similar, this is clearly an area that would benefit greatly from more focused research efforts.

Explore whether or not risk factors vary between hard of hearing persons and persons who are d/Deaf.

The reality that hard of hearing individuals are members of two cultures, mainstream and subculture, functions to place them at greater risk for exposure to criminal elements. This study suggests that the Hard of Hearing may face a greater risk of victimization and be more conflicted about where to go for assistance. Only 35 hard of hearing students were captured by this survey, and as such, it is impossible to examine that population independently from their d/Deaf counterparts. However, preliminary data suggests that this is an area of great need, and this researcher recommends that future research be undertaken to address the unique challenges presented by studying the hard of hearing population.

An extension of this recommendation would be to differentiate between hard of hearing persons who have a life-long condition and those who are hard of hearing as a result of aging. Research suggests that the elderly face a disproportionate vulnerability to victimization. Does that increase with the added vulnerability of diminished hearing? How are their unique circumstances and societal roles handled by the criminal justice system? Do they receive better assistance because they are, for the most part, accepted as members of the mainstream?

Examine the unique issues presented when members of a minority subculture (i.e., American Indian, Amish, etc) are also Deaf.

As minority groups already represent a subgroup of society, how much does deafness increase their social isolation? How prevalent is deafness in minority populations? And do the rates of victimization for minority d/Deaf mirror the existing findings regarding minority victimization experiences? These questions posed involve a much larger exploration into social dynamics and exceed the scope of this project, but they are important ones and offer direction for further research.

Explore the implications and applicability of this research on other non-verbal communities.

This study has argued that one survey instrument is insufficient for addressing the unique needs of all persons with disabilities, citing that the nature of the individual condition dictates that different instruments be used. However, it is unclear whether or not one survey instrument could be used to investigate non-verbal communities as a whole. For example, could the same document be used with persons who use alternative augmentative communication boards? persons with apraxia? persons who are non-verbal as a result of stroke, cerebral palsy, autism, etc.? Are the factors that contribute to the victimization of persons who are Deaf the same for other non-verbal communities?

Explore further the rate at which d/Deaf are victimized by other d/Deaf

Contemporary victimization literature places significant emphasis on factors that increase one's exposure to criminal elements, for instance, the equivalent group and proximity hypotheses. Current criminological theories are exploring the apparent links between criminal victimization and criminal offending. Sparks (1982) has even suggested that offenders are attractive targets for crime because they can be victimized with little chance of legal consequences. Therefore, the answers promised by a culturally sensitive exploration into how often Deaf are victimized by other Deaf have critical application to the development of policies and programs geared towards reinforcing one's ability to maintain a safe existence and should definitely be addressed in any future research efforts.

This area of inquiry is particularly interesting since the instant study indicates that persons who are Deaf face a greater vulnerability from hearing persons. If in fact these preliminary findings are accurate, then policy and prevention programs must address the apparent target selective practices of potential offenders, and further exploration using a rational choice framework is dictated.

Conclusion

This research effort began and ended with a desire to provide empirical data supporting the position that has long been held by professionals who work with the Deaf and Hard of Hearing populations – that being that persons who are Deaf are disproportionately victimized and have little say in their recovery, mainly because of their devalued placement in society. This project not only succeeded in identifying specific areas of weakness, but also uncovered many more areas that need attention.

For example, the finding that the greatest risk to the Deaf for victimization is from hearing offenders is contrary to what was expected, given the tenets of the proximity hypothesis or equivalent group hypothesis. And yet, the finding is replicated in other minority, sub-cultural communities such as the American Indian population, wherein "two-thirds or more of the American Indian victims of robbery, aggravated assault, and simple assault report the offender as belonging to a different race" (Greenfield and Smith, 1999). This suggests that a phenomenon is developing within ostracized communities of intense cultural loyalty that defies traditional theories of crime behavior and results in a virtual taboo of inter-group assault. This is not to say that it doesn't happen, but it doesn't appear to occur at the rate mainstream believes it does.

Additionally, while the findings in this report regarding the rates of violent crimes perpetrated (Table 5.8) against Deaf students varied between two and 20 times greater than the national average (Table 5.7); existing anecdotal data regarding victimization of persons with disabilities has consistently estimated the figures to be as high as 50 times greater than mainstream society.

And finally, this report and its findings offer mainstream society, in general, and criminal justice professionals, specifically, a blueprint for change. Constituent involvement and active participation is vital to the successful development and implementation of programs and policies aimed at equalizing the administration of justice. The beneficiaries are not only the Deaf community but every minority, sub-culture that exists under the umbrella of American society. This is not only an opportunity; it is an obligation and a responsibility.

Appendix A: Gallaudet Research Institute Demographic Profile

2001-2002 REGIONAL AND NATIONAL SUMMARY
Gallaudet Research Institute, 800 Florida Avenue, NE, Washing, DC 20002
202-651-5575 ; 1-800-451-8834 ext 5575

Deaf & Hard of Hearing Students 18 years of age and older (N = 4108)

Sex

	Northeast N	%	Midwest N	%	South N	%	West N	%	Nation N	%
Total Students	688	100.0%	945	100.0%	1504	100.0%	971	100.0%	4108	100.0%
Information NOT reported	3	.4%	3	.3%	8	.5%	11	1.1%	25	.6%
Total Known Information	685	99.6%	942	99.7%	1496	99.5%	960	98.9%	4083	99.4%

	Northeast N	%	Midwest N	%	South N	%	West N	%	Nation N	%
Total Know Information	685	100.0%	942	100.0%	1496	100.0%	960	100.0%	4083	100.0%
Male	373	54.5%	518	55.0%	843	56.4%	525	54.7%	2259	55.3%
Female	312	45.5%	424	45.0%	653	43.6%	435	45.3%	1824	44.7%

RACE/ETHNIC BACKGROUND

	Northeast N	%	Midwest N	%	South N	%	West N	%	Nation N	%
Total Students	688	100.0%	945	100.0%	1504	100.0%	971	100.0%	4108	100.0%
Information NOT reported	10	1.5%	12	1.3%	14	.9%	18	1.9%	54	1.3%
Total Known Information	678	98.5%	933	98.7%	1490	99.1%	953	98.1%	4054	98.7%

	Northeast N	%	Midwest N	%	South N	%	West N	%	Nation N	%
Total Known Information	678	100.0%	933	100.0%	1490	100.0%	953	100.0%	4054	100.0%
White	317	46.8%	629	67.4%	654	43.9%	367	38.5%	1967	48.5%
Black/African American	136	20.1%	139	14.9%	490	32.9%	63	6.6%	828	20.4%
Hispanic	154	22.7%	58	6.2%	268	18.0%	363	38.1%	843	20.8%
American Indian	0	.0%	5	.5%	9	.6%	33	3.5%	47	1.2%
Asian/Pacific Islander	37	5.5%	75	8.0%	29	1.9%	104	10.9%	245	6.0%
Other	24	3.5%	16	1.7%	23	1.5%	11	1.2%	74	1.8%
Multi Ethnic	10	1.5%	11	1.2%	17	1.1%	12	1.3%	50	1.2%

2001-2002 REGIONAL AND NATIONAL SUMMARY
Gallaudet Research Institute, 800 Florida Avenue, NE, Washing, DC 20002
202-651-5575 ; 1-800-451-8834 ext 5575

AGE AT ONSET OF HEARING LOSS (Annual Survey)

	Northeast		Midwest		South		West		Nation	
	N	%	N	%	N	%	N	%	N	%
Total Students	688	100.0%	945	100.0%	1504	100.0%	971	100.0%	4108	100.0%
Information NOT reported	21	3.1%	26	2.8%	48	3.2%	34	3.5%	129	3.1%
Total Known Information	667	96.9%	919	97.2%	1456	96.8%	937	96.5%	3979	96.9%

	Northeast		Midwest		South		West		Nation	
	N	%	N	%	N	%	N	%	N	%
Total Known Information	667	100.0%	919	100.0%	1456	100.0%	937	100.0%	3979	100.0%
At birth	311	46.6%	388	42.2%	611	42.0%	370	39.5%	1680	42.2%
Under 3 years	131	19.6%	134	14.6%	338	23.2%	183	19.5%	786	19.8%
3 years or older	44	6.6%	48	5.2%	96	6.6%	51	5.4%	239	6.0%
Unknown	181	27.1%	349	38.0%	411	28.2%	333	35.5%	1274	32.0%

Appendix B: Consent Documents

(for both students who were Deaf and hearing)

PLEASE DETACH AND KEEP FOR YOUR INFORMATION

Dear Student:

Criminal Justice System and Deaf Americans how it work for both you.

With Letter is questions asking about crime experiences, what situation crime, if you report crime, and if justice system fair to handle your situations with crime.

YOU DECIDE YES OR NO IF YOU WANT TO FILL OUT THE QUESTIONS. **DO NOT** WRITE YOUR NAME ON QUESTIONS SHEET. If you pick yes you want to fill out question sheet, you answer questions and put in box when you finish. **If** you want results of project, you must contact me ask for information about results.

I promise your answers will not show/identify who you are. National Crime Victimization Survey, I compare all answers to questions sheet. Government ask hearing people same questions about crime every six months. Government do not ask deaf people before.

Information is finished with questions. I put all answers in computer. Information used to find how police and courts can improve help for deaf. Information hope use for develop training and awareness program for police, courts, criminal justice system. For example, judges, lawyers, and victim help services. Other ways your questions sheet and information can help. Possible new jobs for deaf, money for programs and policy rules focusing on help deaf people, more ways for deaf to get help from victim recovery program.

YOU DECIDE YES OR NO IF YOU WANT TO FILL OUT THE QUESTIONS. YOUR CHOICE TO FILL OUT QUESTIONS. IF YOU DECIDE NOT TO ANSWER SOME QUESTION THAT OKAY. IF YOU DECIDE YES ANSWERING QUESTIONS YOU CAN STOP ANY TIME.

If you feel not comfortable while fill out questions sheets, please tell Lauren or Kerri. We will call someone to come talk to you. Student Services know about this questions sheets. Student Services can help you. You can contact them at 585-475-2261.

More information you want to know about your rights because you help with questions sheets, and can contact Office of the Associate Provost at John Jay College, Dr. Martin Wallenstein by phone 212-237-8364 or address mail at 899 Tenth Avenue, New York, NY 10019.

Thank you for thinking about helping with project. Without help from you, important area of crime hard for justice system to see.

Sincerely,

Lauren M. Barrow
Ph.D. Candidate
John Jay College of Criminal Justice
lbarrow@earthlink.net

PLEASE DETACH AND KEEP FOR YOUR
INFORMATION

Dear Student:

I am looking at the criminal justice system and how it responds to the needs of Deaf Americans during their experience of a crime.

Attached to this letter is a questionnaire that asks some questions about your possible experiences with crime, the situation surrounding the crime, your choice to report the crime and how you feel the justice system handled the incident(s).

I am asking that you look over the questionnaire and ONLY IF YOU CHOOSE TO DO SO, complete it and deposit it into the box when you are finished. **DO NOT WRITE YOUR NAME ON THE QUESTIONNAIRE.** The results of this project can be made available to you upon completion if you contact me requesting the information.

Your answers will be put into a computer and will be looked at to find out how the police and courts can do a better job. It is hoped that the information will be used to <u>develop training and awareness programs</u> for members of the criminal justice system, i.e.: victim service providers, prosecutors, judges. Other possibilities include new <u>career opportunities</u> for the deaf, <u>money</u> from Justice agencies for new programs and policies focusing on the deaf, <u>greater access</u> for the deaf to victim recovery programs, etc.

I guarantee that your responses will not be identified with you personally. I plan to compare the responses to this questionnaire to the findings of the National Crime Victimization Survey, which are questions that the government asks hearing people every six months.

Completing this questionnaire is COMPLETELY VOLUNTARY. You may choose to participate or not participate. Feel free to skip any questions you do not want to answer. If you do choose to participate, you may stop at any time.

If you experience any discomfort while completing the questionnaire, please tell Lauren or Kerri, and we will immediately get you someone to talk to. If you feel you need more regular assistance, the Student Services office knows about this questionnaire and is available to provide additional services. They can be reached at 585-475-2661.

If you wish any further information regarding your rights as a research participant, you may contact the Office of the Associate Provost at John Jay College, Dr. Martin Wallenstein by phone at 212-237-8364 or by mail at 899 Tenth Avenue, New York, NY 10019.

Thank you for your consideration of this very important project. Without the help of people like you, critical areas of needed improvement within our justice system remain difficult to identify.

Sincerely,

Lauren M. Barrow
Ph.D. Candidate
John Jay College of Criminal Justice
lbarrow@earthlink.net

PART ONE

(11 questions)

Personal Background Information

1. Are you:

    _____ Deaf   _____ Hard of Hearing   _____ Hearing

    If Deaf, are you:

    ____ Oral Deaf   ____ ASL Deaf

2. Are you a member of the Deaf culture?

    _____ Yes   _____ No

3. What is your sex / gender?

    _____ Female   _____ Male

4. What is your birth YEAR?   19 _____

5. On a scale of 0 – 4, how much do you fear becoming a crime victim, (i.e.: having personal things stolen? Being attacked? Getting robbed?)

Never		Sometimes		All the time
0	1	2	3	4

6. Have you been a victim of a crime **since January, 2002**?

    _____ Yes   _____ No   _____ Don't Know

    _____ Can't remember   _____ don't want to discuss this

7. Have you **been a victim** of a crime since you were **12 years old**?

    _____ Yes   _____ No   _____ Don't Know

    _____ Can't remember   _____ don't want to discuss this

Part ONE   Page 1

8.   Are you married now?   _____ Yes   _____ No

        Are you widowed now?   _____ Yes   _____ No

        Are you divorced now?   _____ Yes   _____ No

        Are you separated now?   _____ Yes   _____ No

        Are you single now?   _____ Yes   _____ No

        Do you have a life partner?   _____ Yes   _____ No

               They are   ?   _____ Male   _____ Female

9.   Which of the following census categories best describes your primary ancestry or ethnic origin?

               _____ White (not of Hispanic origin)
               _____ Black / African American (not of Hispanic origin)
               _____ Asian or Pacific Islander
               _____ Hispanic
               _____ Other - _____

10.   Please estimate your total yearly household income:

               _____ Less than $20,000
               _____ $20,000 - $39,999
               _____ $40,000 - $59,999
               _____ $60,000 - $79,999
               _____ $80,000 - $99,999
               _____ More than $100,000

11.   I have: (please check **all** that apply)

               _____ trouble seeing things
               _____ trouble walking
               _____ trouble learning things
               _____ legs or arms that don't work right
               _____ trouble thinking about things
               _____ Schizophrenia or depression
               _____ OTHER: _____
               _____ NONE

PART TWO

(15 questions)

Criminal Justice System

This section will ask you general questions about the criminal justice system

1. If you are a <u>victim</u>, do you have to hire your own lawyer?

          YES   NO   DON'T KNOW   DON'T UNDERSTAND

2. The Judge is supposed to pick who he/she believes before the trial begins.

          TRUE   FALSE   DON'T KNOW   DON'T UNDERSTAND

3. If the police do something wrong in their investigation, the information they collected might not be included in the trial?

          TRUE   FALSE   DON'T KNOW   DON'T UNDERSTAND

4. The prosecutor may also be called a district attorney, or a county attorney, the state's attorney, or a U.S. attorney, depending on where they work.

          TRUE   FALSE   DON'T KNOW   DON'T UNDERSTAND

5. For behavior to be bad or illegal, laws must be written down first. These laws must tell what punishment is for bad behavior. This <u>must be done</u> before it can be a crime.

          TRUE   FALSE   DON'T KNOW   DON'T UNDERSTAND

6. If police arrest you, you are guilty.

          TRUE   FALSE   DON'T KNOW   DON'T UNDERSTAND

7. If you are a victim, you have the right to have someone help you during the trial.

          TRUE   FALSE   DON'T KNOW   DON'T UNDERSTAND

8. If you are a victim of a robbery, no one can help you get your money back.

          TRUE   FALSE   DON'T KNOW   DON'T UNDERSTAND

9. If the person who broke the law (criminal) is plea bargaining, the case is decided without a judge or jury making the decision. Usually, the victims are asked by the lawyers on what they think is a fair punishment for the offender.

TRUE   FALSE   DON'T KNOW   DON'T UNDERSTAND

10. What does the prosecutor do?

_____ tries to defend offender in court
_____ tries to prove offender guilty
_____ tries to arrest offender on street

11. What is a "felony"?

_____ way to go free
_____ very serious crime
_____ person who talks in court

12. What is a penitentiary?

_____ group home
_____ school
_____ prison

13. What does it mean to be acquitted?

_____ offender go jail
_____ offender go free
_____ offender go back to court

14. If the person who broke the law (criminal) is found guilty, who won the case?

_____ prosecutor
_____ victim
_____ defense

15. Who do you call to report a crime?

_____ 911
_____ 411
_____ a relay operator
_____ don't know

PART THREE

(13 crime questions)

Victimization

This section will ask personal questions
about crime

Since Jan 2002, did someone force you to watch movies, pictures or videos showing the sex act (with adults, children or both in the movie) when you didn't want to?

_____ Yes _____ No

If "YES", please answer questions below;

If "NO", please go to page 3.

How many times did this happen since January 2002?

_____ Once
_____ Several (2-5 times)

_____ Many (6-10 times)
_____ Regularly (more than 10 times)

Who showed you the sexual movies, pictures or videos?

____ Mother
____ Sister
____ Boyfriend
____ Family friend (Male - female)
____ School Worker (Male - female)
____ Don't know

_____ Father
_____ Brother
_____ Girlfriend
___ Counselor (Male - female)
_____ Stranger (Male - female)
_____ Don't want to tell

____ Aunt
____ Grandmother
_____ Cousin (Male - female)

____ Uncle
____ Grandfather
____ Neighbor (Male -female)
____ Teacher (Male - female)
____ Driver (Male-female)
____ Other:_____

Where did you see the sexual movies, pictures and videos?

_____ Home
_____ On way to school
_____ At a friend's house

_____ School
_____ On way home
_____ Other: _____

Do you think this happened because you are Deaf?

_____ Yes _____ No

Part THREE

Page 1

After the incident(s), did you tell anyone about what happened? (check all that you told)

_____ I did not tell anyone	_____ told a family member
_____ told a friend	_____ told a staff member or counselor
_____ told a police officer	_____ told a priest, minister or rabbi
_____ Other: _____ (who?)	_____ I don't want to tell who I told

If not, why didn't you tell? (check all that apply)

_____ Scared or Embarrassed	_____ Didn't know how to tell
_____ Didn't think police would care	_____ Didn't think anyone would believe me
_____ Didn't think it was a big deal	_____ Didn't know who to tell
_____ Didn't want person to get in trouble	_____ Other: _____ (what?)

CIRCLE ONE

If you told someone, was your complaint ever investigated by the police?	Yes	No	Don't know, no one told me
If the police investigated, was someone arrested?	Yes	No	Don't know, no one told me
If someone was arrested, were they deaf?	Yes	No	Don't know, no one told me
If someone was arrested, were you interviewed by the state's lawyer?	Yes	No	Don't know, no one told me
If someone was arrested, did the person admit guilt and get a punishment?	Yes	No	Don't know, no one told me
If someone was arrested, did the case go to court?	Yes	No	Don't know, no one told me
If case did go to trial, was the person found guilty?	Yes	No	Don't know, no one told me
If the person was found guilty, did they go to jail?	Yes	No	Don't know, no one told me

Since January 2002, did someone touch your sexual organs (penis, vagina or breasts) **without asking you?**

_____ Yes   _____ No

If "YES", please go to page 4;

If "NO", please answer questions below.

If this has not happened in the past year, has it EVER happened to you?

_____ Yes   _____ No

When? What year? _____

Do you know anyone who this happened to?

_____ Yes   _____ No

If yes, who?

____ Mother	____ Father	____ Aunt	___ Uncle
____ Sister	____ Brother	____ Grandmother	___ Grandfather
____ Friend (Male - female)	____ Cousin (Male - female)	___ Neighbor (Male -female)
____ Family friend (Male - female)	____ School Worker (Male - female)	___ Driver (Male-female)
___ Don't want to tell	____ Other:_____

Did they tell the police?

_____ Yes   _____ No   _____ Don't know

If no, what advice did you give them?

_____ do not tell anyone   _____ tell a family member
_____ tell a staff member or counselor   _____ tell a police officer
_____ tell a priest, minister or rabbi   _____ Other: _____ (who?)

Please go to page 7.

Part THREE   Page 3

How many times did this happen since January 2002?

    _____ Once   _____ Many (6-10 times)
    _____ Several (2-5 times)   _____ Regularly (more than 10 times)

Who touched your penis, vagina or breasts?

___ Mother	___ Father	___ Aunt	___ Uncle
___ Sister	___ Brother	___ Grandmother	___ Grandfather
___ Boyfriend	___ Girlfriend	___ Cousin (Male - female)	___ Neighbor (Male -female)
___ Family friend (Male - female)		___ Counselor (Male - female)	___ Teacher (Male - female)
___ School Worker (Male - female)		___ Stranger (Male - female)	___ Driver (Male-female)
___ Don't know		___ Don't want to tell	___ Other:_____

Please check where this happened?

    _____ Home   _____ School
    _____ On way to school   _____ On way home
    _____ In your bed   _____ In a van or car
    _____ Outdoors   _____ At a friend's house
    _____ Other: _____ (please tell where)

Do you think this happened because you are Deaf?

               _____ Yes   _____ No

After the incident(s), did you tell anyone about what happened? (check all that you told)

    _____ I did not tell anyone   _____ told a family member
    _____ told a friend   _____ told a staff member or counselor
    _____ told a police officer   _____ told a priest, minister or rabbi
    _____ Other: _____ (who?) _____ I don't want to tell who I told

If not, why didn't you tell? (check all that apply)

    _____ Scared or Embarrassed   _____ Didn't know how to tell
    _____ Didn't think police would care   _____ Didn't think anyone would believe me
    _____ Didn't think it was a big deal   _____ Didn't know who to tell
    _____ Didn't want person to get in trouble _____ Other: _____ (what?)

CIRCLE ONE

If you told someone, was your complaint ever investigated by the police?	Yes	No	Don't know, no one told me
If the police investigated, was someone arrested?	Yes	No	Don't know, no one told me
If someone was arrested, were they deaf?	Yes	No	Don't know, no one told me
If someone was arrested, were you interviewed by the state's lawyer?	Yes	No	Don't know, no one told me
If someone was arrested, did the person admit guilt and get a punishment?	Yes	No	Don't know, no one told me
If someone was arrested, did the case go to court?	Yes	No	Don't know, no one told me
If case did go to trial, was the person found guilty?	Yes	No	Don't know, no one told me
If the person was found guilty, did they go to jail?	Yes	No	Don't know, no one told me

For each of the remaining 11 questions (listed below), the format of the sub-questions was exactly the same as the one immediately prior to this one. Instructions were provided in bold, colorful print and where appropriate, pictures were used, i.e.: stop signs for "stop". As mentioned in the text however, the drawback to this format was that the final survey document came to 49 pages, which may very well have created survey fatigue thereby impacting the findings.

Since January 2002, did someone rub or massage your sexual areas (penis, vagina or breasts) without asking you?

Since January 2002, did someone force you to put your mouth on their sexual organs (penis, breasts or vagina)?

Since Jan 2002, did someone put something in your vagina or rectum (penis or object) without asking you?

Since January 2002, did someone <u>steal</u> something that belonged to you and <u>hurt you to get it</u>?

Since January 2002, did someone attack you (i.e., punch or kick) and hurt you (i.e., cuts, bruises, broken bones)?

Since January 2002, did someone <u>attack</u> <u>you with a weapon</u> (i.e., baseball bat, rock, gun, knife, etc)?

Since Jan. 2002, did someone <u>steal</u> something <u>from you without hurting you,</u> (i.e.,: purse, backpack, laptop etc)?

Since Jan. 2002, did someone <u>steal</u> something from <u>inside</u> your home when you weren't home, (i.e.,: jewelry, TV, computer, stereo, etc)

Since Jan. 2002, did someone <u>steal</u> something from <u>outside</u> your home without you knowing, (i.e.,: bike)?

Since January 2002, did someone <u>steal</u> your car or motorcycle?

Since January 2002, did someone sign your check and take your money?

Bibliography

----, (1987). *Gallaudet Encyclopedia of Deaf People and Deafness* (Three Volume Set). McGraw-Hill Professional.

----, (1998). Proceedings of the first world conference on mental health and deafness. Gallaudet University, Washington, DC. Retrieved from <//mhdeafintl.gallaudet.edu/ proceedings1/proc1toc.htm>

Adler, F; Mueller, G.O.W. and Laufer, W. (1998) *Criminology*. New York: McGraw Hill.

Allen, T. (1986). Academic achievement among hearing impaired students: 1974-1983. In A. Schildroth & M. Karchmer (eds.), *Children in America* (pp. 161-206). San Diego, CA: Little Brown & Company.

Allison, S.R. & Vining, C.B.. (1999). Native American Culture and Language. *Bilingual Review, 24* (1-2), 193-207.

Alston, P. (2001). Special Issue Spirituality and Disability. *Journal of Rehabilitation, 67* (1), 3.

Anderson, P. R. & Newman, D. J. (1998) *Introduction to Criminal Justice. 6th Edition.* New York, NY: McGraw Hill.

Anello, B. (1998). Report for the DAWN Ontario Board from the Inter-Sectoral Workshop on Violence Against Women with Disabilities and Deaf Women and Access to the Justice System, November 27, 1998. North Bay, Ontario.

Babbidge, H. D. (1965). *Higher Education Act of 1965: Hearings before the Subcommittee on Education of the Committee on Labor and Public Welfare, U.S. Senate, 89th Congress.* Washington D.C.: U.S. Government Printing Office.

Baladerian, N. (1991). Sexual abuse of people with developmental disabilities. *Journal of Sexuality and Disability, 9,* (3), 96-101.

Balint, Kathryn. (2000, February 29). An equal voice: For those with disabilities, computing is a 'lifeline'. *The San Diego Union-Tribune*; p. 6.

Barrow, L. (1998). [Disabled / differently-abled crime victim on-line survey]. Unpublished materials.

Baum, Ph.D., K. & Klaus, P. (2005). *Violent Victimization of College Students, 1995-2002.* Washington, DC: Bureau of Justice Statistics, Special Report. NCJ 206836.

Blue, Amy V., Ph.D., (2005, April 2). *The Provision of Culturally Competent Health Care* Charleston, SC: MUSC College of Medicine.

Boncheck, M. S., Hurwitz, R., & Mallery, J. (1996). Will the Web democratize or polarize the political process? A White House electronic publications survey. *World Wide Web Journal, 1 (3)*. Retrieved from <//www.w3j.com/3/s3.bonchek.html>.

Bone, T.A., (1998). Insiders in a Deaf world: Barriers for the Deaf Offender in the Hearing Criminal Justice System. Thesis submitted to the faculty of the Graduate Studies of the University of Manitoba, CANADA.

Branson, J. & Miller, D. (2002). *Damned for Their Difference : The Cultural Construction of Deaf People as Disabled.* Washington, DC: Gallaudet University Press.

Brantingham, P.J. & Brantingham, P.L. (1981). *Environmental Criminology.* Beverly Hills, CA: Sage Publications.

Bronfenbrenner, U. (1977). Toward an experimental ecology of human development. *American Psychologist, 32*, 513-531.

Brookhauser, P.E., Sullivan, P., Scanlan, J.M., & Gabarino, J. (1986) Identifying the sexually abused deaf child: The otoaryngologist's role. *Laryngoscope, 96*: 152-8.

Brouner, J. (2001). Look Again: Domestic violence and disability for communities against rape and assault. Retrieved from <www.cara-seattle.org/w_look.html>.

Burch, S. (2001) Reading between the signs: Defending Deaf culture in early Twentieth-Century America. In P.K. Longmore. and L. Umansky (eds). *The New Disability History: American Perspectives.* (pp. 214-235). New York: New York University Press.

Chough, S.K. (1983). The trust vs. mistrust phenomenon among deaf persons. Readings in deafness, Monograph 7. In D. Watson, K. Steitler, P. Peterson & W.K. Fulton, (eds). *Mental health, substance abuse and deafness.* (pp. 17-19). Silver Spring, MD: American Deafness and Rehabilitation Association.

Clapton, J. (1996) "Disability, Inclusion and the Christian Church", Paper presented at Disability, Religion and Health Conference, Brisbane, October 18-20, 1996.

Clarke, Ronald R. (ed.) (1997). *Situational Crime Prevention: Successful Case Studies, 2nd ed.* New York: Harrow and Heston.

Clarke, R. & Cornish, D.B. (1985). Modeling offenders' decisions. *Crime & Justice, 6:* 152.

Clarke, R. & Felson, M. (2004). Introduction: Routine Activity and Rational choice. In R.V. Clarke and M. Felson (Eds.), Routine Activity and Rational Choice (*Advances in Criminological Theory, 5*). New Brunswick, NJ: Transaction Publishers.

Cohen, L.E., & Felson, M. (1979) Social change and crime rate trends: A routine activity approach. *American Sociological Review, 44*: 588-608.

Cole, S. (1984) Facing the challenges of sexual abuse in persons with disabilities. *Sexuality and Disability, 7(3 /4)*: 71-87.

Cornish, D., & Clarke, R.V. (Eds.) (1986) *The reasoning criminal.* New York, NY: Springer-Verlag.

Cornish, D.B., (1994) Crimes as Scripts. In D. Zahm & P. Cromwell (Eds.), *Proceedings of the International Seminar on Environmental Criminology and Crime Analysis, University of Miami, 1993* (pp. 30-45). Tallahassee: Florida Criminal Justice Executive Institute.

Costello, Ph.D., E. (1994). *American Sign Language Dictionary.* New York: Random House.

Croteau, R. (2006, August 25). Deaf Woman Files Suit Against New Braunfels. *The San Antonio Express-News.* p. 3B.

Crouch, R. A. (1997). "Letting the deaf be Deaf: Reconsidering the use of the cochlear implants in prelingually deaf children." *Hastings Center Report, 27(4)*: 14-21.

Dakwa, K. (2001). The Kallikak Family. Retrieved from: <www.indiana.edu/~intell/ kallikak.shtml>

Decker, I. (1997). Lesson: Research Sampling. Retrieved from <www2.nau.edu/~mezza/ nur390/Mod3/sampling/lesson.html>

Desloges, P. (1779). *Observations d'un sourd et muet sur 'Un Cours élémentaire d'éducation des sourds et muets,' publié en 1779 par M. l'abbé Deschamps.* Amsterdam and Paris: Morin. As cited in Harlan Lane (ed) and Franklin Philip, translator. (1984). *The Deaf Experience: Classics in language and education,* (Gallaudet Classics in Deaf Studies Series, Vol. 5).

Devine, H.A. & Briggs, C. (2001). Domestic violence & disabled women. *NY City Voices.* Retrieved from: <www.newyorkcityvoices.org/jun01g.html>.

DisAbled Women's Network. (1998). Violence against women with disabilities. Toronto online.

Doe, T. (1997, December 1). Violence tops agenda for women with disabilities. *Contemporary Women's Issues Database :14.*

Duvall, J. (1992). *Law Enforcement & the Deaf.* Ohio: Sharp Image.

Duvall, J. (1988, September). Sexual Abuse of Deaf Children: Incident, Investigation and Interviewing. Paper presented at the World Conference on Modern Investigation, Organized Crime and Human Rights, South Africa.

Evans-Pritchard, E. (1937). *Witchcraft, Oracles and Magic amongst the Azande.* Oxford: Clarendon Press.

Everington, C.T. and Luckasson, R. (1992). *Competency Assessment to Stand Trial for Defendants with Mental Retardation (CAST-MR).* International Diagnostic Systems, Inc.

Fagan, J., Piper, E., & Cheng, Y. (1987). Contributions to victimizations to delinquency in Inner Cities. *Journal of Criminal Law and Criminology, 78*: 286-300.

Fallahay, J. (2000). *The Right to a Full Hearing: Improving Access to the Courts for People Who Are Deaf or Hard of Hearing.* Des Moines, IA: American Judicature Society.

Farwell, R.M. (1976). Speech reading: A research review. *American Annals of the Deaf. 121*(1): 18-22.

Fattah, E.A. (1991). *Understanding criminal victimization.* Englewood Cliffs, NJ: Prentice Hall.

Fattah, E.A. (1993). The rational choice/opportunity perspectives as a vehicle for integrating criminological and victimological theories. In R.V. Clarke and M. Felson (Eds.), Routine Activity and Rational Choice (*Advances in Criminological Theory, 5).* New Brunswick, NJ: Transaction Publishers.

Felson, M., & Clarke, R.V. (1998) Opportunity makes the thief: Practical theory for crime prevention. *Police Research Series, 98.* For the Policing and Reducing Crime Unit of the Research, Development and Statistics Directorate for the Home Office, England. <www.homeoffice.gov.uk/rds/prgpdfs/fprs98.pdf>.

Fink, A. (1995). *How to ask survey questions.* Thousand Oaks, CA: SAGE Publications.

Finkelhor, D., Hotaling, G., Lewis, I. and Smith, C. (1990) Sexual Abuse in a national survey of adult men and women: Prevalence, characteristics and risk factors. *Child Abuse & Neglect, 14*:19-28.

Finkelhor, D. (1986). *A Sourcebook on child sexual abuse.* Beverly Hills, CA: Sage Publications.

Fisher, B. S., Cullen, F. T. & Turner, M. G. (2000). *The sexual victimization of college women.* Washington, DC: Bureau of Justice Statistics, NCJ 182369

French-American Foundation. (1994). *Parallel views: Education and access for deaf people in France and the United States.* Washington, DC: Gallaudet University Press.

Friedrich, W.N. & Boriskin, J.A. (1978). Primary prevention of child abuse: Focus on the special child. *Hospital and Community Psychiatry, 29(*4), 248-256.

Freud, S. (1896). The Aetiology of Hysteria. In J. Strachey (ed.), *Complete Psychological Works, Standard Edition, Volume 3* London: Hogarth Press.

Fry, E. (1987). *Disabled People and the 1987 General Election.* London: Spastics Society.

Gallaudet Research Institute. (January, 2003). *Regional and National Summary Report of Data from the 2001-2002 Annual Survey of Deaf and Hard of Hearing Children & Youth.* Washington, DC: GRI, Gallaudet University.

Galvin, R. (2003). The Making of the Disabled Identity: A linguistic analysis of marginalization. *Disability Studies Quarterly, 23* (2): 149-178.

Gavin, K. (2003). Heading back to campus? Watch for depression triggered by college stresses, U-M expert advises. University of Michigan Health Minute, retrieved from <www.med.umich.edu/ opm/newspage/2003/college depression.htm>.

Gilbride, S. (online) The disabled and domestic violence. Retrieved from <www.rochestercdr.org/Domestic ViolenceText.html>.

Goddard, H. H. (1917). Mental tests and the immigrant. *Journal of Delinquency, 2*, 243-277.

Goddard, M.A. (1989). *Sexual Assault: A hospital/community protocol for forensic and medical examination.* Rockville, MD: National Criminal Justice Reference Service.

Greenberg, M.T., Domitrovich, C. & Bumbarger, B. (2001). The Prevention of Mental Disorders in School-Aged Children: Current State of the Field. *Prevention & Treatment, 4,* (1). Retrieved from <//journals.apa.org/prevention/ volume4/pre0040001a.html>.

Greenfeld, L.A. and Smith, S.K. (1999). *American Indians and crime.* Washington, DC: Bureau of Justice Statistics, Special Report. NCJ 173386

Greenwood, P.W., & Petersilia, J.R. (1975). *The criminal investigation process, Vol. I: Summary and policy implications.* Santa Monica, Calif.: RAND Corporation. Retrieved from: <www.rand.org/pubs/reports/R1776>.

Gregorie, T. (1994). "Differently-abled Victims of Crime." In *Focus on the Future: A Systems Approach to Prosecution and Victim Assistance* (Chap-8). Arlington, VA: National Victim Center.

Groce, N.E. (1999). Disability in Cross-Cultural Perspective: Rethinking Disability. *The Lancet. 354,* (9180), 756-757.

Guthmann, D. (2000). An analysis of variable that impact treatment outcomes of chemically dependent Deaf and Hard of Hearing individuals. Deaf Health Network. Retrieved from <www.deafvision.net/deafhealth/a/cd/ cd06.htm>.

Haller, B. (1999). Media history and disability. *Clio, 4* (2).

Halpern, C. A. (1997). Listening in on Deaf Culture. Retrieved from <www.nev8.com/text/1-01/deaf_txt.html>.

Hendershot, G. (2001, December 12). Internet use by people with disabilities grows at twice the rate of non-disabled, yet still lags significantly behind. Retrieved from <www.nod.org>.

Herrenkohl, E.C., & Herrenkohl, R.C. (1981). *Explanations of child maltreatment: A preliminary appraisal.* Center for Social Research, National Conference for Family Violence Researchers. Durham: New Hampshire University.

Hindelang, M., Gottfredson, M., & Garafolo, J. (1978). *Victims of personal crime: An empirical foundation for a theory of personal victimization.* Cambridge, MA: Ballinger.

Hitchens, C. (2006, August). The Vietnam Syndrome *Vanity Fair, 552,* 106-111.

Hobbes, T. (1651) *Leviathan.*

Holcomb, T., & Peyton, J. K. (1992). *ESL Literacy for a linguistic minority: The deaf experience.* Retrieved March 31, 2004 from <www.cal.org/caela/digests/ ESL_ LITERACY.HTML>.

Holt, J. and Hotto, S. (1994). *Demographic Aspects of Hearing Impairment: Questions and Answers.* Washington, DC: Gallaudet University. Retrieved October 15, 1997 from <www.gallaudet.edu/~cadsweb/factshee.html>.

Hoog, C. (2003). Model protocol on safety planning for domestic violence victims with disabilities. Abused Deaf Women's

Advocacy Services (ADWAS). Retrieved from <wscadv.org/Resources/protocol_disability_safety_planning.pdf>.

Hough, M. & Mayhew, P. (1983). *The British Crime Survey: First report.* London: Her Majesty's Stationary Office.

Houtenville, A. J. (2005). Disability Statistics in the United States. Ithaca, NY: Cornell University Rehabilitation Research and Training Center, retrieved from <www.disabilitystatistics.org>.

Jeffrey, C.R. (1971). *Crime prevention through environmental design.* Beverly Hills, CA: Sage.

Joseph, J.M., Sawyer, R., Desmond, S. (1995) Sexual knowledge, behavior and sources of information among Deaf and Hard-of-Hearing college students. *American Annals of the Deaf, 140* (4), 338-345.

Kannapel, B. (1983). The trust vs. mistrust phenomenon among deaf persons. Readings in deafness, Monograph 7. In D. Watson, K. Steitler, P. Peterson, & W.K. Fulton (eds). *Mental Health, substance abuse and deafness.* (pp. 20-22) Silver Spring, MD: American Deafness and Rehabilitation Association.

Karmen, A. (1996). *Crime victims: An introduction into victimology, 2nd ed.* Belmont, CA: Wadsworth Publishing Company.

Karmen, A. (2001). *Crime victims: An introduction into victimology, 4rth ed.* Belmont, CA: Wadsworth Publishing Company.

Kilpatrick, D., Best, C., Veronen, L., Amick, A., Villeponteaux, L., and Ruff, G. (1985). Mental health correlates of criminal victimization: A random community survey. *Journal of Consulting and Clinical Psychology 53 (6),* 866–873.

King, C.M. & Quigley, S.P. (1985). *Reading and deafness.* San Diego, CA: College-Hill Press.

Knutson, J. & Sullivan, P. (1993). Communicative disorders as a risk factor in abuse. *Topics in Language Disorders, 13* (4), 1-14.

Krogh, K.S. & Lindsay, P.H. (1999). Including people with disabilities in research. *Augmentative and Alternative Communication, 15* (4), 222-233.

Lane, H. (1984). *When the Mind Hears.* New York, NY: Random House, Inc.

Lane, H. (1992) *The Mask Of Benevolence: Disabling the Deaf Community.* New York, NY: Knopf

Larkin, M. (undated) "What is social constructionism?" retrieved from <www.psy.dmu.ac.uk/michael/ soc_con_disc.htm>

Lashley, J.R. (1989). Drinking routines/lifestyles and predatory victimization: A causal analysis. *Justice Quarterly, 6*: 4.

LeBeau, J. & Castellano, T. (1987). *The routine activity approach: An inventory and critique* (unpublished manuscript) Carbondale, Ill: Center for the Studies of Crime, Delinquency, and Corrections, Southern Illinois University.

Liachowitz, C. (1988). *Disability as a social construct.* Philadelphia, PA: University of Pennsylvania Press.

Lipton, Ph.D., D.S., Goldstein, Ph.D., M.F., Fahnbulleh, III, F.W. & Gertz, E.N. (1996) The Interactive Video-Questionnaire: a new technology for interviewing deaf persons. *American Annals of the Deaf, 141* (5), 370-8.

Locke, J. (1689). *Two Treatises on Government*

Macionis, J.J. (2001). *Sociology, 8th ed.* Upple Saddle River, NJ: Prentice Hall.

Mapp v. Ohio, 367 U.S. 643 (1961).

McNeil, J.M. (1995) Employment and poverty rates from the 1994 and 1995 CPS. Derived from unpublished tabulations, U.S. Bureau of the Census. Employment rates from the 199093 CPS, *Poverty in the United States* series of reports published by the U.S. Bureau of the Census. Accessed. April 03, 2005.

Mendelsohn, B. (1963) The Origin of Victimology. *Excerpta Criminologica, 3*: 239- 256.

Mertens, D. M. (1996). Breaking the Silence About Sexual Abuse of Deaf Youth. *American Annals of the Deaf, 141* (5), 352-358.

Miles, M. (1995). Disability in an Eastern religious context: historical perspectives. *Disability and Society, 10* (1).

Miranda v. Arizona, 384 U.S. 436 (1966).

Mitchell, R. E. (2004). "How many deaf people are there in the United States?". <gri.gallaudet.edu/ demographics/deaf-US.php>

Moriarty, L. J. (2002). *Policing and victims.* Upper Saddle River, NJ: Prentice Hall.

Morrone, C., RN. (2001). Helpful hints on talking to angels. *NursingSpectrum,* retrieved from </community.nursing spectrum.com/MagazineArticles/article.cfm?AID=3831>

Mullins, J.B. (1986). The relationship between child abuse and handicapping conditions. *Journal of School Health, 56* (4), 134-36.

Nagi, S. Z. (1969). *Disability and rehabilitation.* Columbus, OH: Ohio State University Press.

Najavits, L.M., Gastfriend, D.R., Barber, J.P, et al . (1998). Cocaine dependence with and without PTSD in the NIDA cocaine collaborative study. *American Journal of Psychiatry,155,* 214-219.

National Cued Speech Association (NCSA). Cued speech discovery: What is cued speech. <www.cuedspeech.com/whatis.asp>.

National Institute on Deafness and Communication Disorders (NIDCD): A Report of the Task Force on the National Strategic Research Plan. (1989). *Federal Register 57:* 33063.

Neisser, A. (1983). *The other side of silence: Sign language and the Deaf community in America.* New York, NY: Knopf.

Newman, O. (1972). *Defensible space.* New York, NY.

Nosek, M.A., Howland, C., Rintala, D.H., Young, M.E., Chanpong, G.F. (2001) National study of women with physical disabilities: Final report. *Sexuality and Disability, 19* (1), 5-40.

Obinna, Ph.D., M.S.S.W., J. (2005). Researching sexual violence in the Deaf community. *Sexual Assault Report, 8* (3), 33-48.

Oliver, M. (1990). *The politics of disablement: A sociological approach.* New York, NY: St. Martin's Press.

Outlaw, M. S., Ruback, R. B., & Britt, C. (2002). Repeat and multiple victimizations: The role of individual and contextual factors. *Violence and Victims. 17,*187-204.

Papert, S., Idit Harel (ed.). (1990). *Introduction: Constructionist Learning.* Cambridge, MA: MIT Media Laboratory.

Pease, K., (1994) Crime prevention. In M. Maguire, R. Morgan, and R. Reiner (eds.), *Oxford handbook of criminology (1ˢᵗ ed.).* (pp. 659-703). Oxford: Clarendon Press.

Race, J. (2005) "Deaf Nationalism" *Prospect, Issue 108.* retrieved from <www.prospect-magazine.co.uk>

Reason, P. (1994). Three Approaches to Participative Inquiry. As cited in N.K. Denzin and Y.S. Lincoln, (eds.). *Handbook of qualitative research.* Thousand Oaks, CA: SAGE Publications, Inc.

Reiss, A. J., & Roth, J. A. (1993). *Understanding and preventing violence.* Washington, D. C.: National Academy Press.

Resnick, M.D. (1984). The social construction of disability. In R.W. Blum (ed.) *Chronic illness in childhood and adolescence.* (pgs: 29-46). Orlando, FL: Grune & Stratton.

Reyna, P. (undated) *Confronting domestic violence in the Deaf community.* Training materials from the Los Angeles Commission on Assaults Against Women, LACAAW.

Rivers-Moore, B. (1992). *Family violence against women with disabilities.* Retrieved 10/16/00 from: www.hc-sc.gc.ca/hppb/familyviolence/womendiseng.html.

Roberson, C. (1994). *Introduction to criminal justice.* Placerville, CA: Copperhouse Publishing Company.

Rowe, C. (2005, March 26) Building refuge for battered deaf women: North Seattle project will house victims of domestic violence. *Seattle Post-Intelligencer.*

Sacks, O. (1989). *Seeing voices: A journey into the world of the deaf.* NY: Harper Perennial.

Sadusky, J. & Obinna, J. (2002). Violence against women: Focus groups with culturally distinct and underserved communities. A report to the Wisconsin Department of Health and Family Services. Minneapolis, MN: Rainbow Research.

Safilios-Rothschild, C. (1970). *The sociology and social psychology of disability and rehabilitation.* New York, NY: Random House.

Sampson, R.J., & Lauritsen, J.L. (1990). Deviant lifestyles, proximity to crime, and the offender-victim link in personal violence. *Journal of Research in Crime and Delinquency, 27,* 110-139.

Schafer, S. (1968). *The victim and his Criminal: A study in functional responsibility.* New York, NY: Random House.

Schein, J.D. and Delk, M.T. (1974). *The Deaf population of the United States.* Silver Spring, MD: National Association of the Deaf.

Schemo, D.J. (2006, Oct. 31). At University for the Deaf, Protesters Press Broader Demands. *New York Times.*

Schroedel, J.G. (1984). Analyzing surveys on Deaf adults: Implications for survey research on persons with disabilities. *Social Science Medicine, 19* (6), 619-627.

Selway, D. & Ashman, A.F. (1998). Disability, religion and health: A literature review in search of the spiritual dimensions of disability. *Disability and Society, 13,* (3), 429-441.

Senn, C.Y. (1988). *Vulnerable: Sexual abuse and people with an intellectual handicap.* Ontario, Canada: G. Allan Roeher Institute.

Shaffer, J. N., & Ruback, R. B. (2002). The relationship between violent victimization and violent offending in juvenile. *Research*

Bulletin. Washington, DC: Office of Juvenile Justice and Delinquency Prevention. NCJ 195737.

Shaw, A. (1995). Social constructionism and the inner city: Designing environments for social development an urban renewal. Retrieved from <//lucy.media.mit.edu/ ~acs/chapter1.html>.

Shaw, C. & McKay, H. (1942) *Juvenile delinquency in urban areas.* Chicago, IL: University of Chicago Press.

Sherman, L.W., Gartin, P.R. and Buerger, M.E. (1989). Hot spots of predatory crime: Routine activities and the criminology of place. *Criminology, 27* (1), 27-55.

Singer, S. (1981). Homogeneous victim-offender populations: A review and some research implications. *Journal of Criminal Law and Criminology, 72*, 779.

Small, S. (1995). Action-oriented research: Models and methods. *Journal of Marriage and the Family, 57* (4), 941-952.

Smith, S.J. (1982). Victimization in the inner city. *British Journal of Criminology, 22*, 386-402.

Sobsey, D. (1991). Patterns of sexual abuse and assault. *Journal of Sexuality and Disability, 9 (3),* 243-259.

Sobsey, D. (1994) *Violence and Abuse in the lives of people with disabilities: The end of silent acceptance?* Baltimore, MD: Paul H. Brooks Publishing Co.

Sobsey, D. & Doe, T. (1991) Patterns of sexual abuse and assault. *Sexuality and Disability, 9* (3), 243-259.

Sorenson, S.B., Siegel, J.M., Golding, J.M., & Stein, J.A. (1991). Repeated Sexual Victimization. *Violence and Victims, 6* (4), 299-308.

Sparks, R.F. (1982). *Research on victims of crime.* Washington, D.C.: Government Printing Office.

Sparks, R. F., Genn, H. & Dodd, D. (1977). *Surveying victims: A study of the measurement of criminal victimization, perceptions of crime and attitudes to criminal justice.* New York, NY: John Wiley.

Spector, K. (2002, November 12). Activists learn of deaf people's fight for jobs. OH: Plain Dealer Reporter

Sullivan, P. M., Brookhouser, MD, P.E., Knutson, Ph.D., J.F., Scanlan, MD, J.M., Schulte, Ph.D., L.E. (1991) Patterns of physical and sexual abuse of communicatively handicapped children. *Annals of Otol Rhinol Laryngol, 100,* 188-194.

Sullivan, P.M., and Knutson, J.F. (1998). The Association between child maltreatment and disabilities in a hospital-based epidemiological study. *Child Abuse & Neglect, 22* (4), 271-288.

Sullivan, P. M., Scanlan, J.M. & LaBarre, A. (1986) *Characteristics and therapeutic issues with abused deaf adolescents.* Presentation at Second National Conference on Habilitation and Rehabilitation of Deaf Adolescents, Afton, Oklahoma.

Sullivan, P. M., Vernon, M., & Scanlan, J.M. (1987) Sexual abuse of deaf youth. *American Annals of the Deaf, 132* (4), 256-262.

Sutherland, E. H. (1937). *The professional thief.* Chicago, IL: University of Chicago Press.

Swan. (February, 1987). As cited in P. Sullivan, M. Vernon and J. Scanlan Sexual abuse of deaf youth. *American Annals of the Deaf, 132* (4), 256-262.

Swisher, M.V. (1989). The language learning situation of deaf students. *TESOL Quarterly, 23,* 239-257.

Terry v. Ohio, 392 U.S. 1 (1968).

Trickett, A., Osborn, D.R., Seymour, J., & Pease, K. (1992). What is different about high crime areas? *British Journal of Criminology, 32,* 81-89.

Tucker, B. (1991) *The Feel of Silence.* Philadelphia, PA: Temple University Press.

Tutty, L.M., Rothery, M.A., and Grinnell, R.M. Jr. (1996). *Qualitative Research for Social Workers.* Needham Heights, MA: Allyn and Bacon.

Union of the Physically Impaired Against Segregration (UPIAS). (1975). Fundamental Principles of Disability. London: UPIAS.

U.S. Department of Education, National Center for Education Statistics. (2005). Projection of Education Statistics to 2014. (NCES 2005-074). Table 11

U.S. Department of Education, National Center for Education Statistics. (2005). *Digest of Education of Statistics, 2004* (NCES 2006-005) Table 206. (nces.ed.gov/fastfacts/display.asp?id+98)

Van der Kolk, B.A. (1989). The compulsion to repeat the trauma: Re-enactment, revictimization and masochism. *Psychiatric Clinics of North America, 12* (2), 389-411.

Von Hentig, H. (1948) *The criminal and his victim: studies in the sociobiology of crime.* New Haven, CT: Yale University Press.

Vygotsky, L. (1978). *Mind in Society: The Development off Higher Psychological Processes.* Cambridge, MA: Harvard University Press.

Web-for-all, The Importance of the Internet for Disabled People. Retrieved from <//www.webforall.info/html/englisch/_bedeutung_des_internet.php>.

Whatley, J. (2000) Violence against women with disabilities: Policy implications of what we don't know. *Impact, 11* (3), 4.

White, J. and Cho, D. (2003) A social norms intervention to reduce coercive sexual behaviors among Deaf and Hard-of-Hearing college students. *The Report on Social Norms, 2* (4).

Williams, L.M., & White, J.A. (2001) *Violence against women in a cultural context.* Paper presented at the Training and Technical Assistance Institute for Grantees in the U.S. Department of Justice Campus Grants to Combat Violent Crimes against Women, October 2001.

Williams, R.M., Jr. (1970). *American society: A sociological interpretation, 3ʳᵈ ed.* New York, NY: Alfred A. Knopf.

Wooster, Ann, K., J.D., Annotation, *When Are Public Entities Required to Provide Services, Programs, or Activities to Disabled Individuals Under Americans with Disabilities Act, 42 USCA § 12132,* 160 ALR Fed 637 (2000)

Worthington, G. M. (1984). Sexual exploitation and abuse of people with disabilities. *Center for Women Policy Studies, March/April,* 7-8.

Young, M.E., Nosek, M.A., Howland, C., Chapong, G., & Rintala, D.H. (1997). Prevalence of abuse of women with disabilities, *Archives of Physical Medicine and Rehabilitation, 78* (12), 34-38.

Young, A. (2001). Reflections on validity and epistemology in a study of working relations between deaf and hearing professionals. *Qualitative Health Resources, 11* (2), 179-89.

Index